Praise for the first edi
Assets From A Texas Divorce and the authors:

"When it comes to divorce Texas style, Mr. Vanden Eykel is the reigning king...he is the divorce-law Jedi."

The Dallas Morning News

"As I read this book, I felt like I was listening to a trusted friend, who is also a highly experienced family lawyer."

Jane Klafter, Allen

"A high-profile divorce in the Lone Star State is likely to have a 'Gunfight at the O.K. Corral' quality to it...."

Houston Chronicle

"I recommend this book to any lawyer involved in the area of family law."
William W. Harris, Judge, Texas 233rd Judicial District

"The professional, yet compassionate approach to divorce in Texas makes this book a wonderful way to access sound legal advice at a fraction of an hourly attorney's fee."

Amazon.com

"I actually read this cover to cover. How interesting!"
KTBC Channel 7, Austin

"*(Protecting Your Assets From A Texas Divorce)*...is intended to help individuals prepare financial information...."
McKinney Messenger

PROTECTING YOUR ASSETS FROM A TEXAS DIVORCE

Ike Vanden Eykel   Rick Robertson
Heather King   Charla Conner

Attorneys at Law

Protecting Your Assets From A Texas Divorce
Ike Vanden Eykel, Rick Robertson,
Heather King, Charla Conner

PSG Books
9603 White Rock Trail, Suite 310   Dallas, Texas 75238
214/340-6223
info@prosolutionsgroup.com

Books published under the PSG Books imprint are distributed to the U.S. book trade by Midpoint Tradebooks. Resellers outside the book trade who wish to purchase books in quantity at a discount may contact PSG Books at 214/340-6223.

Contact authors Ike Vanden Eykel (Ike@koonsfuller.com), Rick Robertson (Rick@koonsfuller.com), Heather King (Heather@ koonsfuller.com), Charla Conner (Charla@koonsfuller.com) to speak to groups on the financial aspects of divorce. For scheduling, contact Kim Hyde (Kim@koonsfuller.com) at the law firm of Koons, Fuller, Vanden Eykel & Robertson, P.C., 5700 W. Plano Parkway, Suite 2200, Plano, Texas 75093, phone 972/769-2727, www.koonsfuller.com.

ISBN-13: 978-0-9749461-4-6
Manufactured in the United States of America

8 7 6 5 4 3 2 1

Notice and Disclaimer

State laws, legal precedents, tax codes and regulations vary greatly from one jurisdiction to another and change over time. The reader should not use this book for specific legal advice. Every divorce case and post-divorce action is unique, requiring the advice of those versed in the laws of the jurisdiction where the action is taken. It must be understood, therefore, that this book will provide readers with a general overview of financial matters related to the divorce process and post-divorce issues, so they may take legal action or otherwise address these issues better informed.

Reading this book does not establish an attorney-client relationship between the reader and the authors. Consult an attorney for specific information related to your personal situation.

Library of Congress Cataloging-in-Publication Data

Protecting your assets from a Texas divorce / Ike Vanden
Eykel ... [et al.]. -- 2nd ed.
    p. cm. -- (The successful divorce)
  Rev. ed. of: Protecting your assets from a Texas divorce /
Ike Vanden Eykel, Kathryn Murphy, Rick Robertson. c2005.
  ISBN 978-0-9749461-4-6
  1. Divorce settlements--Texas--Popular works. 2. Equitable
distribution of marital property--Texas--Popular works. 3.
Marital property--Texas--Popular works. I. Vanden Eykel,
Ike, 1949- II. Vanden Eykel, Ike, 1949- Protecting your
assets from a Texas divorce.
  KFT1300.V36 2009
  346.76401'664--dc22

                      2009027254

TABLE OF CONTENTS

About the Authors...13

Part One
Contemplating Action

Chapter 1
Hope for the Best, Prepare for the Worst......................19
Divorce Can Cause Financial Hardship • Divorce Stats • The Financial Truths of a Texas Divorce • Consider Reconciliation • Staying Together for the Kids? • Planning Your Divorce

HE SAID, SHE SAID:
Two Looks At A Marriage

Chapter 2
In An Uncertain Economy, Divorce Is More Difficult........38
Cash Problems Lead Stress Parade • Business Values Vary • Collaborative Divorce Can Save A Business • Everyone on Economic Scale Affected

Chapter 3
What Kind of Divorce Will This Be?...................................48
Can Your Spouse Remain a Friend? • Gain Access to Information • Seven Simple Steps to Prepare for Divorce • Think Strategically

Chapter 4
With or Without An Attorney..55
Representing Yourself • Sharing One Attorney • The Importance of a Specialist • Initial Interviews • Questions to Ask Your Attorney • Guarantees vs. Experience

Chapter 5
Collaborative Law...**68**
A Paradigm Shift in Family Law • If Settlement Fails, Attorneys Must Withdraw • Locate a Collaborative Lawyer

HE SAID, SHE SAID:
A More Humane Method

Chapter 6
Save Money on Legal Fees.....................................**77**
Educate Yourself • Contingency Fees • 10 Effective Strategies for Controlling Legal Fees

Chapter 7
Work Toward Settlement.......................................**82**
What Is Fair? • Major Financial Blunders • Most Cases Settle • The Importance of Mediation • The Benefits Are Significant • Beware of Mediation Abuse • The Role of Your Attorney in Resolving Disputes

Chapter 8
Handling Temporary Matters...............................**92**
Temporary Restraining Orders • Temporary Orders • Protective Orders • Contested Temporary Hearings

HE SAID, SHE SAID:
To Her a Drunk, To Him a Loving Dad

Chapter 9
Finances in the Short Term.................................**101**
Use of Joint Accounts • Joint Credit Card Debt • Paying Bills During the Case

Chapter 10
Discovery...**104**

Hiding Money, Finding Assets • Make an Inventory • Formal Discovery • Interrogatories • Request for Production of Documents • Request for Admissions • Depositions • Electronic Evidence

Chapter 11
Financial Planning..**114**
14 Suggestions for Your Financial Security

Chapter 12
Other Professionals Your Attorney May Enlist................**119**
Other Legal Specialists • Accountants • Estate Planners • Appraisers • Business Valuation Experts • Mental Health Professionals

Chapter 13
Couples Living Together..**129**
Common Law or Just Unmarried? • Children of the Unwed • Proving Paternity Now Easier

12 Steps to a More Productive Divorce

Part Two
Dividing Assets and Debts

HE SAID, SHE SAID: It's Her Separate Property

Chapter 14
Dividing Assets at Divorce...**142**
Identify Your Assets • Community Property or Separate Property? • What Is Your Property Worth? • The Property Division • Letting the Court Decide • Dividing Assets in a "Just and Right" Manner

Chapter 15
Dealing with the Family Home at Divorce........................**153**
Sell the Home and Divide the Equity • Determine Net Equity in Your Home • Appoint a Receiver to Sell Your Home • Transfer Interest in Your Home from One Spouse to the Other • Temporary

Use by One Spouse • When a Judge Must Decide • Consider Your Housing Options • Tax Matters Related to a Home • Play It Safe: Do a Title Search

HE SAID, SHE SAID:
Who Can Afford the Family Home?

Chapter 16
Dividing the Family Business...**168**
Who Gets the Business? • Valuing the Business • Favored Business Entities • Tax Liabilities of the Business

HE SAID, SHE SAID: Dental Practice a Major Asset

Chapter 17
Employee Benefits/Retirement and Beyond...........................**183**
Characterization and Division of Assets • Options Not Just For the Wealthy • Orders to Divide Retirement/Employee Benefits • Loans, Taxes and Penalties/Retirement Plans

HE SAID, SHE SAID:
Sometimes Forgotten Assets

Chapter 18
Divorces at a Certain Age..**195**
Social Security Benefits

HE SAID, SHE SAID:
The Ultimate Loss of Identity

Chapter 19
Community Debt and the Impact of Bankruptcy..............**203**
Cataloguing Your Debt • Apportioning Debt • Which Debts Belong to Whom? • Bankruptcy and Its Effect on Community Debts • Alternatives to Bankruptcy

Part Three
Look to the Future

HE SAID, SHE SAID:
No Clear Line between Child Support and Visitation

Chapter 20
Support Your Children..215
Child Support Collection • Calculating Child Support • Special
Circumstances • Pay Child Support through State System • How
Long Do You Pay Child Support?

Chapter 21
Insuring Your Health and Life..222
Health Insurance for the Children • Health Insurance for Your
Spouse • Life Insurance Protects Future Payments

HE SAID, SHE SAID:
Helping Her Regain Her Balance

Chapter 22
Alimony and Maintenance..231
Limited Eligibility • Types of Alimony • Factors to Consider •
Modifying Alimony • Tax Implications • Impact of Bankruptcy

Comments From Divorcing People
That Make A Family Lawyer Flinch

Chapter 23
Common Tax Issues...239
Prior Year Liabilities or Refund • Who Files Current Year Tax
Return? • Payments and Transfers • Who Gets Dependency
Exemptions? • Retirement Plan Issues • Overpayment of Taxes •
Taxing Closely Held Businesses

Chapter 24
If You Go to Court...**247**
The Family Court Setup in Texas • Your First Court Setting •
Appearing in Court • Courtroom Cast of Characters • A Trial
Docket Primer • Judge or Jury Best in Property Cases? • Keep
Composed on the Stand • Basic Rules for Giving Testimony

Chapter 25
A Divorce Is Granted...**256**
The Final Decree • Details, Details, Details... • Still Upset? Try an
Appeal

HE SAID, SHE SAID: A National Hot-Button Issue

Chapter 26
Relocating a Child and Other Modifications......................**265**
Relocating a Child • Change of Custody • More or Less Child
Support • Modifying Visitation

Chapter 27
Getting On With Your Life..**272**
When Confronted, Choose Reason • But When Reason Doesn't
Work ...

Chapter 28
Prenups and Postnups:
Anticipating Another Marriage...**277**
What's Protected By a Prenuptial Agreement? • Why a Postnuptial
Agreement? • How to Enforce or Break These Agreements

Chapter 29
Never Again..**282**

Appendices..**284-335**

About the Authors

Ike Vanden Eykel is one of America's top divorce lawyers and author of the regional bestseller, *Lone Star Divorce*. Managing partner of the Southwest's largest family law firm, Koons, Fuller, Vanden Eykel & Robertson, he is board certified in both family law and civil trial law. Ike came to prominence during the 1980s as a champion of fathers' rights, but *Vogue* magazine has named him one of the Top Lawyers for Women in Texas. He has been featured in *Town & Country* magazine as one of America's Top 10 Divorce Lawyers and in *Texas Monthly* as one of the state's Top 100 Attorneys.

Ike has very discreetly represented many rich and famous Texans. After handling an especially contentious divorce for a Park Cities housewife, he was depicted in the book *My Husband Is Trying To Kill Me* and a made-for-TV movie, *Dead Before Dawn.*

Firmly established as one of the true statesmen of Texas family law, Ike was annointed the "reigning king" of Texas divorce and the "divorce-law Jedi" in two separate features on him in *The Dallas Morning News* during 2007.

Besides his publishing triumphs, Ike has built one of the nation's most prized family law boutiques and a brand name in Texas family law. He divides his time among each of four offices throughout North Texas and is scheduled to become president of the Dallas Bar Association in 2010.

Rick Robertson is the newest name partner at Koons, Fuller, Vanden Eykel & Robertson and heads the firm's Plano office. He has been selected a Texas Super Lawyer by *Law and Politics* magazine and has been featured in *Texas Monthly* among the state's most outstanding family lawyers.

He has also been named by *D Magazine* among The Best Lawyers in Dallas and Fort Worth from surveys of his fellow attorneys. He has also been listed in *The Best Lawyers in America* for several years and was featured among *Texas' Best Lawyers* based on evaluations by his peers in 2009.

Rick is a Fellow in the Texas Bar Foundation, a member of the Texas Academy of Family Law Specialists and the College of the State Bar of Texas, a former Director of the Texas Young Lawyers Association and a member of the Collin County, Texas and American Bar Associations.

He has written articles and made presentations on family law issues to local, state and national bar associations. He is considered an expert on the use of electronic evidence in divorce cases and the use of social media.

Rick has appeared often on television and talk radio. He is an accomplished spokesman for his law firm and the book. To learn more about him or the law firm of Koons, Fuller, Vanden Eykel & Robertson, visit www.koonsfuller.com.

Heather King is one of the state's most complete family lawyers. She is one of the few family law specialists who handles divorce and related matters all the way from inception to the appeals court and beyond. She has written extensively on a wide range of family law topics and often speaks to other lawyers on what non-family attorneys need to know about divorce and child custody.

Heather has been president of the Tarrant County Bar Association and has been named one of the top attor- neys in Fort Worth by *Fort Worth Texas* magazine. She has been selected one of the top 100 lawyers in Texas and one of the top 50 female lawyers in the state in surveys of her peers. She was also selected among *Texas' Best Lawyers* by the organization that publishes *The Best Lawyers in America*.

She is manager of the Southlake office of Koons, Fuller, Vanden Eykel & Robertson.

<u>Charla Bradshaw Conner</u> is an avid writer and editor of material on legal topics. Her article in 2007 on the disposition of retirement assets in divorce was selected the most outstanding family law paper of the year by the State Bar of Texas.

She was trained as a psychologist before attending law school. She practiced in a small firm in Denton before merging that firm with Koons, Fuller, Vanden Eykel & Robertson and becoming manager of the Denton office. She is board certified in family law by the Texas Board of Legal Specialization and has been selected as a Texas Super Lawyer and one of the top 50 female lawyers in Texas.

Charla is well known throughout North Texas and formerly served as mayor pro tem of Westlake.

Part One
CONTEMPLATING ACTION

"A divorce doesn't end a relationship with your spouse, it simply redefines it. It's a redistribution of power between two parties. The key to success, financially and emotionally, is learning to operate as a divorced couple rather than a married couple. It's a whole new way of living and coping with the issues that will inevitably surface even after your divorce is final. The rules as you once knew them no longer apply."

Rick Robertson
"Yours, Mine And Ours"
D Magazine

CHAPTER 1

HOPE FOR THE BEST, PREPARE FOR THE WORST

IF YOU RECALL, the tragic events of September 11, 2001, were thought to have changed our lives forever. Supposedly, families were brought closer together by it. It was claimed at the time that we stood together as Americans like no other period in recent memory, forsaking such culturally defeating acts as divorce and alienation.

Divorce was down, weddings were up and families were spending more time together. Certainly, we needed to believe that a dramatic shift had taken place during those dark days, but statistical evidence told a different story. In Dallas County, for example, divorce filings actually increased slightly in the fourth quarter of 2001 to 2,819 from a total of 2,786 in the same period of 2000. Marriage applications, on the other hand, were virtually unchanged from one year to the next.

Were most people devoting more time to family together-ness? Actually not. We seemed to be paying more attention to our house pets. Market research conducted nationwide by advertising network Euro RSCG found that 36% of American women who own dogs said they were spending more time with them after September 11 while less than half that number spent more time with their husbands.

So perhaps things didn't change as much as we hoped. Divorce, it seems, is an institution that is always present, no matter what else happens. The incidence of divorce seems to be impervious to acts of God, war or economic uncertainty.

Many people ask us whether economic prosperity or recession encourages divorce the most. We say that divorce is with us whether people are living the good life or suffering through economic hardship. And although divorce fluctuates little because of economic condition, divorce itself can affect your economic status.

"We know what the cause of poverty is in this country and, like it or not, it's divorce and non-wedlock childbearing," says Dr. Steve Nock, a family demographer and professor of sociology at the University of Virginia. "We know that for every three divorces, one family ends up below the poverty line. The average woman with dependent children who ends up in poverty stays poor for eight months. The federal government pays for part of that, but states pay the balance. Divorce, by itself, is a major economic issue."

Divorce Can Cause Financial Hardship

Many people who became adults during the 20-year period when divorce rates were at their highest, from the 1960s through the early 1980s, felt the financial roller coaster of divorce. Those who experienced multiple marriages increased their net worth during marriage and slashed it in half after divorce many times

Divorce Stats

Total divorces granted in the U.S. each year:
1.1 million

State with the lowest divorce rate:
Massachusetts

State with the highest divorce rate:
Nevada

Texas divorce rate (2007):
31st highest in the country

Estimated average length of divorce from start to finish:
1 year

Number of divorced people nationwide:
19.8 million

Number of divorced people in Texas:
1.55 million

Estimated number of children involved in divorce:
1.075 million

Percent of all children living with a divorced parent:
40

Amount spent annually on weddings:
$72 Billion

Amount spent annually on divorce:
$31 Billion

Statistics taken from the U.S. Census Bureau, the Centers for Disease Control, the National Marriage Project and the Texas Department of State Health Statistics.

over. According to a survey published in *Time* magazine in 2005, the average net worth of married couples, ages 51 to 61, is $132,200. Those who are divorced average only $33,700. There is little disagreement about the financial affects of divorce.

There is great disagreement about the emotional costs of such life choices. *The Unexpected Legacy of Divorce* chronicles therapist Judith Wallerstein's 25-year landmark study of 131 children of divorce. Through in-depth personal interviews, Wallerstein centers on the painful search of these "lost" children, now adults, who struggle to overcome the feeling that love and trust are doomed. Equally impressive is the work of researcher and sociologist E. Mavis Hetherington, whose book *For Better or For Worse: Divorce Reconsidered*, was released in 2002. Hetherington tracked nearly 1,400 families and more than 2,500 children. Seventy-five percent to 80% of the children of divorce in her study indicated very little long-term damage from their parents' divorce. The other 20 to 25% of children from divorced families suffered varying social, emotional or psychological problems. This compared with 10% of children from intact families. None of these studies conclude that you can experience a "good" divorce, although Hetherington is far more hopeful that children of divorce can emerge in good health than Wallerstein.

Holding the middle ground in this debate is the book by sociologist Constance Ahrons, *We're Still Family: What Grown Children Have to Say About Their Parents' Divorce*. Of the 173 grown children Ahrons studied, almost 80% felt their parents were better off today and didn't wish their parents were still together. These grown children felt better off or not affected by a long-ago divorce, while 20% had "life-long scars that didn't heal."

The financial impact divorce imposes on divorcing people and their children, as well as their extended families, is not the subject of these studies. Emotional crises can increase financial woes, which generate more emotional upheaval. Before making the decision to divorce, do a reality check to make certain that's really the best course.

Most people facing the financial realities of divorce reach this point without really knowing how much money they have. Some people never actually add up their assets until they must divide them during a divorce. In some instances, these people are astounded by how much money they have accumulated during the marriage. Add the equity in a house to the total of their personal property, the amount in retirement funds and perhaps the value of a business, and a seemingly middle-class family can be worth several million dollars.

Others are stunned at the small amount of money they have from their union. Living in a large home, driving new cars, sending their kids to the best private schools and vacationing several times a year can consume every penny they earn. Often, these couples are left with large debts and few assets.

Divorce can become a money pit for both the payor spouse and the recipient spouse. The payor spouse is the one who may wind up with a business or other assets that cannot be divided and must pay child support or make other payments to a recipient spouse. For the payor spouse, these payments can be devastating. For the recipient spouse, the total payment rarely equals the amount of money that person spent each month before the divorce.

This money once paid for a single household. Now the parties expect the same amount of money to pay for two households. No order of the court can make the money stretch far enough to afford the same lifestyle enjoyed before the divorce for two people in two separate places.

Imagine doubling every expense in your monthly household budget and attempting to pay these bills with the same monthly income. Very few families can shoulder this burden and maintain the same lifestyle without running a serious deficit. Both spouses feel entitled to the savings account, retirement funds and the equity in the family home. And most claim the other created the debts.

The emotional and financial aspects of divorce are intertwined so completely that otherwise fiscally savvy people often become their own worst enemy by the way they resolve a divorce. Some want to get the divorce over quickly. This desire clouds all logic and causes one spouse to accept a poor settlement in an effort to bring closure. Bringing a swift end to the marriage, often leaves at least one of the spouses with a financially insecure future.

On the other hand, one party may be so consumed with the need for revenge that he or she would rather give all the money to lawyers and other professionals than let that "no-good ex" have pocket change to spend when the divorce is over.

Many people have a common misconception that the divorce process will work itself out in a way that is financially fair. But the court can only divide assets according to the law and the evidence, and that is not always fair to both parties.

"I had litigants come into my courtroom wanting me to divide assets with nothing more than their opinion about the value," says Susan Rankin, a former Dallas County family court judge. "If she says their business is worth $600,000, he says it has a negative value and they don't offer expert testimony, I have to rely on my own instinct to determine how much the business is worth and, therefore, how much of the other assets each party receives."

To survive the financial impact of a divorce, the parties should determine their needs and the options available to them. For those who are still deciding whether to divorce or are not certain a spouse is about to file, planning is essential.

A thorough examination of the household budget and needs will help divorcing people reach the most successful financial outcome possible. A study of income sources, expenses, assets and liabilities can suggest the most advantageous division of assets and debts in the divorce.

The Financial Truths of a Texas Divorce

Lone Star Divorce included a list of truths common to all divorces in Texas. The following list is more specific to the financial truths common to every case.

Truth #1: Divorces can be final in as few as 60 days, although very complex divorces and those that go to trial may not be final for months.

Truth #2: Once a divorce is filed and one party wants to go through with it, you can't stop it from happening and your assets will be divided.

Truth #3: Contentious, litigated divorces are more financially devastating than agreed settlements.

Truth #4: Your property may not be divided equally. The judge may look at future earning capacity, fault for the divorce and other criteria when making a disproportionate division.

Truth #5: If one spouse proves that an asset is his or her separate property, the judge must award that asset to that spouse.

Truth #6: Unless you have no significant assets or means to support yourself and you have been married more than 10 years, or you and your spouse agree to it, in most cases there will be no alimony once the divorce is final.

Truth #7: The spouse who does not have primary custody of the children will, in practically every case, pay child support.

Truth #8: If the other side requests your financial information, you will have to comply unless you settle. Even then, the other side may not agree without getting a look at your complete financial picture.

Truth #9: Your spouse can still file for bankruptcy after the divorce, leaving you with the responsibility for certain debts he or she was ordered to pay.

Truth #10: It is difficult to reopen a case or prevail on appeal, so get everything you possibly can from the property settlement the first time around.

Consider Reconciliation

Just for a moment, look at your chances to reconcile and keep your marriage together. Strictly from a financial standpoint, staying married usually is your most productive alternative. So if there is any way you can overcome your differences and keep your family intact, you owe it to yourself and your children to explore the possibilities.

Studies indicate that money is the number one factor in the breakup of marriages in Texas and in every other jurisdiction. It's telling that divorce has increased dramatically in the post-World War II era of unbridled prosperity in this country. The more money you have, it would seem, the more you have to quarrel about. In pre-war America, men worked and made the money while women stayed home and cared for the kids. Since men made the money, they usually determined how that money would be spent.

Today, with a prevalence of two-income households, the use of family funds often involves reaching common ground over an endless series of purchases.

Often, disagreements are so intense and persistent that the two parties fail to quell them. Nerve endings are left raw by financial decisions, especially in an economic downturn. Should I pay the electric bill or buy that new pair of shoes? Did you remember to pay property taxes or that expensive ticket you got for speeding in a school zone? And how on earth can we afford private school and select soccer at the same time?

Some of these questions involve major decisions of lifestyle and purpose, affecting you and your children's future. To solve these problems, you may need the services of a therapist or psychiatrist. You may have to deal with personal traits such as selfishness or insecurity.

Dr. Maryanne Watson, a board-certified family psychologist in Plano, a suburb of Dallas, says that in her experience, people fight most about money, kids and sex. "It really boils down to their problem-solving skills and how they make decisions— especially financial decisions," Dr. Watson says. "If you do not have enough money to pay your bills, that puts a tremendous strain on the relationship. Then, everything is argued about, from buying clothes for the children to how much you spend on groceries. Everything becomes a potential argument."

For some problems, a financial advisor can look at the overall picture and allocate resources, instructing the parties to pay taxes and bills before splurging on luxuries. In this new economic environment, it may take someone like this to make one spouse or the other understand some hard financial realities. Just because you went to an exclusive private school doesn't mean your children can attend the same school, if you don't have the money.

For those in dire financial straits, many churches offer counseling. These sessions may be at a reduced rate or even free to those who don't know where to turn. Making a few painless financial compromises can save many thousands of dollars and years of grief.

Staying Together for the Kids?

In the 1950s, a controversial notion held that people should stay together for the children. That was a time when divorce was rare. After so many divorces over the past three decades, we realize that divorce is not a short-term fix for marital problems. It is emotionally draining and may create more financial problems than the marriage itself.

Make sure to prepare for the process and become aware of the opportunities to save the marriage. Before proceeding with a divorce, exhaust every available avenue to avoid it. Each community has a network of religious advisors, marriage counselors and support groups. Discuss your uncertainty with close friends. If you have children, talk to divorced parents to determine the pros and cons of their situations. Good information can help you make the right decision.

Big life decisions, such as whether to stay married or get divorced, need to be made when you are feeling calm and centered, after you have taken as much time as you need to explore the options.

Most therapists and marriage counselors believe you should only stay together for the children if you can maintain a reasonably healthy relationship. "Staying together for the kids can be a real gift to your children," says Dr. Watson, "but sometimes divorce is best for the children. Studies show that those raised in a hostile environment have a higher-than-normal level of stress hormone."

Situations that involve abusive, violent or other unacceptable behavior fall into another category entirely. When there isn't time to seek legal advice, a decision must be made immediately for the safety and the welfare of children. Once that decision has been made, get sound legal counsel and utilize the justice system to prevent further deterioration of the situation.

But a relationship doesn't have to be abusive to be emotionally and financial damaging. In the 1970s and early 1980s, the percentage of first-time marriages that resulted in divorce peaked at about 65%. Fortunately, those percentages have fallen over the past decade. The reasons for the decrease are twofold: fewer people are getting married (as a percentage of the population), and those who marry are waiting until later in life, when they are more mature and can shoulder the responsibility better. That maturity seems to have reduced the number of marriages that end on a whim.

Our experience is that people are looking at divorce more realistically these days. They seem to be more able to assess the downside of divorce, so that when they make a decision to divorce it is from an informed position and not because of a silly spat.

Still, about 43 % of first marriages end in divorce. That's still a lot of anger and confusion, both emotionally and financially. When people feel that way, few things are more cathartic than making a decision. At some point you may have to stop the discussion and settle things once and for all. For most people, making that decision is scary but liberating. You know money will be tight. Taking care of your family will be more difficult. And having to sift through the financial details of your life with this person will not be fun. By making the decision to divorce, though, you take your fate into your own hands.

Planning Your Divorce

Divorce planning is a whole new occupation that centers on smoothing over financial bumps at the end of marriage. You may be more familiar with the job of the wedding planner, who fusses over details of how many ushers and bridesmaids to outfit, what kind of groom's cake to order and where to place flowers in the chapel. The work of the divorce planner is certainly not as romantic, but it is equally important to the continued happiness of the parties.

Divorce planners are usually financial planners or analysts with experience helping people cope with the vagaries of divorce and its financial aftermath. Some of these professionals earn the relatively new designation of certified divorce planner, while others are financial planners or wealth managers. Divorce planners advise people to collect financial information and organize it before seeing an attorney.

There is a difference between planning and taking calculated steps to hide or dispose of assets. Planning is good. If you move into divorce with little forethought, you may be setting yourself up for a lifelong disaster. Considering the dire consequences of inaction, assertive action will help you achieve a successful financial divorce. Hiding assets, on the other hand, will inevitably get you into big trouble.

One of the most interesting features of family law is seeing how two parties perceive the same set of circumstances. Throughout this book, we provide you with narratives about specific subjects indicating what the husband said about the marriage and divorce, what the wife said about the same events and how the issue was settled or dealt with in court.

In this first HE SAID, SHE SAID account, follow the evolution of a marriage and divorce, along with an actual result.

HE SAID SHE SAID: Two Looks At A Marriage

He said she was a dynamic, productive contributor to society ... until a few minutes after they married seven years ago. At that moment, she developed an overwhelming sense of entitlement and spent her days at the mall, having cocktails with the girls and furnishing their home in a way that overspent her household allowance. They never intended to have children and so he encouraged her to go back to work by keeping a tight rein on her spending. When he realized she was not going to get a job, he increased the pressure to keep her from running up credit card bills that only he would pay.

He worked hard, at first, to maximize the profit from his oil consulting business. He enjoyed his work. It allowed them the freedom to snorkel off the Cayman Islands and spend the summer in Colorado. They went to Europe twice the first year they were married, and the money just seemed to flow.

But it was never enough for her. She berated him in front of his friends and family. Called him cheap. Accused him of loving golf and his business more than her. She rarely planned a meal and didn't want to entertain anyone he enjoyed. She put on weight. At one of the last dinner parties they gave, she told their stunned friends there was no way she would ever work again because no self-respecting woman over the age of 40 would be caught dead with a job. She spent more and more time away from him, with her own family. Her sister even told him she had a sexual affair with a handsome friend of her parents.

In the last few years, he began to slow down the pace of his business. He was nearing retirement age. Why work so hard, he thought, when she failed to contribute one dollar or an ounce of comfort to his life? Because he worked less, his earnings fell. But their combined spending did not decrease.

Once he began to understand that their relationship was not going to change, he started to make provisions for the possibility that they might not live their entire lives together. He had come into the marriage with several million dollars, including stocks, bonds, oil leases and real estate. Property owned before the marriage normally is not subject to division by the court, as are increases in the value of these properties. The only property they owned together was a lovely home in the Park Cities of Dallas that they bought the year they married.

When he needed money, he simply refinanced the house, which continued to rise in value during the marriage. He preserved his separate property while they spent most of their community assets.

As he came to realize that divorce was certain, he cut back on her allowance. He wanted her to get the idea that he wasn't paying for everything anymore. Perhaps she would feel the need for money and finally get a job.

She said he was a cheapskate, a liar and a thief. From the moment they married, he was on her case. He nagged her for spending too much money and not spending enough time with him. He complained that she was overweight, although he always wanted to eat lavish meals in restaurants and he had gained weight himself.

Before the marriage, she said, things were different. He came on like a high roller, carrying wads of cash and buying her whatever she wanted. He told her she would never want for anything as long as she was with him. She was his princess, his trophy wife and never once before they married did he talk about her working outside the home.

How could she possibly have a career anyway? She had to follow him around the world. Her work was to impress his friends and family. He was really married to the golf course and he expected her to be a dutiful golfing wife. She tried hard to like that lifestyle, but he always compared her to the wives of his golfing buddies. She wasn't any good at the game or waiting around while others played it, no matter how hard she tried. And when he criticized her, she went further into her shell.

They went to golf courses all around the world. To finance his obsession, he skimped on furnishings for their home and held her to an impossibly low household budget. Since she felt so out of place with his friends, she spent time with her own friends and family. He resented that and his resentment played havoc with her self-esteem. She enjoyed the compliments of a family friend. But her sister was jealous of her and told her husband that she and the man were having an affair. Nothing could have been further from the truth.

It was about this time that she noted a difference. He stopped criticizing her and just fell silent. He began to talk about divorce, but she just shrugged him off. If she could get him to forget about divorce, maybe things could be like they were at the start. He began to conserve his money. He wasn't flashing it around or buying her things. He took business trips by himself and didn't ask her to go. She didn't know what was worse–his criticism or ignoring her.

She tried to get into his financial records. She was sure he was hiding money somewhere, perhaps in an offshore account. They refinanced the house and then the money was gone. They had reached the end.

The result was a divorce after seven years. As you can see, love was not a major component of their relationship. Because they had no children, the division of property was the major issue. He had been very careful, since early in the marriage, to keep his separate property separate, and didn't commingle any income from that property.

She thought there would be plenty of money to divide. He knew they had spent most of their community assets, but he didn't want to leave her penniless. That was before they started throwing accusations at each other.

She accused him of cruelty. He shot back that she was an adulteress. She was certain he was hiding assets from her and she ran up legal bills looking for hidden money, but found none. As a healthy woman in her mid-40s who held a good job before the marriage, she would be able to work and rebuild her assets.

The steady appreciation in the value of their home provided the only divisible asset. He decided to give her all the furnishings in the home, as well as some of his separate property, as an inducement to ratify the property settlement.

She walked away with those furnishings, her personal belong-
ings, two oil leases and approximately $100,000 in cash. Her
attorney fees totaled $97,000. After the bills were paid, she
had $3,000 cash and would receive about $2,000 a month
from the oil leases.

It was time for her to go back to work.

CHAPTER 2

IN AN UNCERTAIN ECONOMY, DIVORCE IS MORE DIFFICULT

DIVORCE CAN BE MESSY ENOUGH, even in the best of times. Families flush with cash haggle over who gets to keep the house. They negotiate business values and calmly consider assets as bargaining chips in the to and fro of breakup economics.

Then comes an economic meltdown and all hell breaks loose. Neither of the parties wants a house that has lost much of its value.

The worth of a family business is related to how many employees you can fire and the amount of expenses you can cut. A bad economy turns an anxious process into a feeding frenzy. Without a clear-cut recovery, the waters continue to be murky.

Cash Problems Lead Stress Parade

Studies indicate that money is the major cause of stress in a marriage. You might think it would be sex, children, even in-laws. But no, it's money. As divorce lawyers, we are often asked if marital breakups are more difficult in good times or bad. While there is really no evidence to suggest that the overall number of divorces changes with the Dow Jones average, keeping up with that crop of Joneses gets a lot more difficult when times are bad.

In our practice, we've seen that divorcing people face far more complex situations when there aren't enough assets to go around. Two thousand eight was a challenging year for people in a variety of industries. Our partner, Julie Crawford, was hired in January 2008 to represent a woman whose husband was deeply involved in the oil and gas business. Four-dollar-a-gallon gasoline was affording this couple a sumptuous lifestyle. The husband spent into six figures on a birthday party. He was flying around the world in his private jet well into the summer.

Then in early fall, the bottom dropped out of the market. While most of the country's population smiled at lower gas prices, the oil and gas man faced the reality of his situation. He needed to restructure his business, selling off equipment and laying off people.

"He had been spending the money he made like there was no tomorrow," Julie says, "but tomorrow came quickly."

The downturn was so sudden that Julie hired an expert in oil and gas to evaluate the situation and make certain they were getting the right numbers.

"My client figured her estranged husband had to be cooking the books," Julie recalls. "Just two months before, he was in his private jet. Now he couldn't afford the fuel. We studied the situation and saw how the value of his business had decreased in no time at all. It really demanded every bit of creativity we could muster to come to an agreement."

Business Values Vary

Typically, the owner of a family business (usually the husband) wants his spouse to make their financials work by reducing household spending, while the other spouse (usually the wife) wants the man to downsize his business to bridge the shortfall. Both parties must begin to grasp the reality of the situation, that the marketplace is shrinking and with it their community holdings. If the attorneys in a divorce are not able to convince their clients that the financial situation is severe, they will call in experts such as family therapists and financial planners to buttress their efforts.

One truism pertains here that applies in good times and bad. If a family is unable to afford one household when they are together, they must make drastic cuts in expenditures to pay for two households when they split up. Even in the best of times, the specter of two mortgages, two cable bills and two places for kids to stay is hard to manage.

Further complicating negotiations is the bursting of the housing bubble, the event that economists say brought on this latest financial downturn. For most Texans, the family home is the greatest asset in their marriage. As the bubble enlarged, they were able to pull equity out of their home to pay off community debts. In the worst-case scenario, they simply put a FOR SALE sign out front and their troubles went away in a matter of days. In many parts of the state, this remedy has become unavailable since the housing bubble burst.

Another of our partners, Mike DeBruin, saw his practice affected by the slump in real estate. He represented the wife of a commercial real estate developer who had seen the value of his holdings decline dramatically. No new projects were in the pipe-line, cash flow was greatly restricted and he was facing the pos-sibility of having to cut his overhead. But this man is a risk-taker, and he worried that his ability to come back from the doldrums would be compromised if he slashed his workforce. In normal times, the couple would simply sell their home to give him the cash to weather the storm.

"A year ago, their home appraised for $2.5 million," Mike says. "Then they had it on the market for $1.8 million, and they weren't getting any takers."

Collaborative Divorce Can Save A Business

One of the most effective ways to save the family business is to take the collaborative law approach. Cheryl Hall, business col-umnist for *The Dallas Morning News*, examined this approach recently in a story titled, "Nasty divorces can mean trouble for businesses, too."

She followed the actions of Koons Fuller partner Kevin Fuller, president of the Collaborative Law Institute of Texas, who was named the Dallas Family Lawyer of the Year for 2009 by a rating service called *The Best Lawyers in America*.

Hard economic times call for creative solutions, Fuller says. He's arranged settlements where the spouse – typically the wife – gets to share in any business recov-ery down the road.

He's also worked out agreements where the owner keeps the business intact while the spouse gets cash, stocks and bonds, and perhaps an alimony package. "The trade-off is: security now for the wife vs. potential upside or disaster for the business owner. People trade for what they most need or want."

Collaborative divorces involve written legal rules. Both parties sign an agreement not to go to court while going through the process, which can be lengthy. But either can opt out at any time. Their attorneys can't represent them if they wind up in court.

In the worst of economic times, Fuller maintained, handling marital disruptions privately is essential.

When large business deals are in the wind, even the hint of divorce can scotch the deal. Fuller had a recent case where a company's initial public offering could have been detonated if the wife's attorneys had deposed investment bankers, big investors and upper management in the company.

"By taking a collaborative approach, the IPO went through and both husband and wife profited millions they might have lost had the case been aggressively litigated," says Fuller, who represented the husband.

That businessman, bound by divorce confidentiality agreements not to publicly disclose his name, says the process was long and arduous but worth it.

"It could have been devastating to the company," the ex-husband says. "It provided an opportunity to keep a private matter private. It could have derailed something much bigger than both of us."

Business owners can get awfully shrewd when their margins begin to thin. They decide to go forward with a divorce they wouldn't attempt in better times, realizing their businesses will never be worth less than they are in this downturn. The less the value of the business, the less they will have to pay their soon-to-be ex.

Everyone On Economic Scale Affected

And it's not just the high rollers who are now on the bottom looking up. Following are 13 valuable tips that are extremely important to anyone divorcing in a difficult economy. Ignore them at your peril. Pay strict adherence to them and you are more likely to insure the financial health of you and your loved ones.

Check your credit *before* filing for divorce.

The downside of community property laws is that half of the *debt* belongs to you, also. You want to check your credit before filing for divorce so that you can make sure your ex has not borrowed money using your name or that debts which belong to your ex aren't on your credit report. A prominent feature of this financial crisis is the unavailability of credit. Those with a clean credit report will have a much easier time buying a home, new cars. etc.

Don't let the judge divide your assets.

Only you know what your assets are worth. If you and your spouse can come to an agreement about the property division, you are certain to emerge with more value, whether that is market value or the more sentimental variety. Judges don't really like to divide assets, so they don't pay as much attention to what you want and how the division will affect your long-term well being.

Make sure your spouse is not hiding assets.

You may ask yourself, "How cynical are these people? Do divorcing people really engage in such practices?" While we prefer to be considered realists, we know from experience that some dishonest people get divorced. A person who is perfectly honest in good times may feel justified in hiding valuable assets when love (and money) have gone away.

Pay off as many jointly held debts as possible or convert them into individual debts.

Even though a family court judge awards a debt to your former spouse, if you are a signatory on the debt you still remain liable for it. An individual creditor can release one of the parties, but most have no incentive to do that until the debt is paid. If one newly divorced person fails to pay a debt that rightly belongs to that party, that creditor wants to be able to come after the other party for the money.

Try to take only the debts that secure assets you receive.

How eager would you be to make payments on the automobile driven by your ex? Likewise, how confident are you that your ex-spouse would make timely payments on the vehicle you drive? Such situations can lead to the repo man and loss of your good credit.

Check your credit *during* and *after* filing for divorce.

The current economic situation is basically a credit crunch caused by bad housing loans. Divorce can play havoc with your credit, and you'll need the best rating possible to buy a house or make other purchases. You'll want to ensure that no bad debts have impacted your credit report or that your spouse has not applied for credit in your name.

Expedite sale of the marital residence.

Foreclosures are increasing, and so is the time period necessary to sell homes. If you have to sell your home to split community assets, make the necessary repairs and improvements to get the job done. Otherwise, you could be left with a home you can't sell.

Don't make your spouse too comfortable in a home you want to sell.

Sometimes one spouse pays the house payment and lets the other spouse stay in the home while the residence is being sold. If you do this, you may need to build in some penalty if your spouse fails to cooperate with your realtor, leaves the house dirty or otherwise keeps the home from selling.

Pay close attention to the last joint income tax return.

If you were divorced before the end of a year, you cannot file a joint tax return with the person to whom you were married.

Make sure the taxes get filed, know what will happen to any refund and decide who is responsible for any tax payments.

Allocate the dependency exemptions for your children.

Whoever claims the children on their taxes can save a lot of money. Usually the person who has primary responsibility for the children retains the exemptions, unless the parties agree otherwise. If having these exemptions won't help you much on your taxes, you may want to use them as a bargaining chip and trade them for something of more value to you.

Make sure the spouse who is to provide the most money is insured.

If you are trying to make ends meet and one of your most important sources of funds is your ex, you may want to take out a life insurance policy on that person. If something happened to your ex at a critical point, you might not be able to withstand the shortfall.

Be realistic about child support payments.

If you anticipate living paycheck to paycheck for some time, adequate child support may be essential. Child support is based on state guidelines, except in the case of very wealthy people. This support should cover the needs of the child but not be so taxing on the paying spouse that he or she defaults on payment.

In difficult economic times, courtesy and cooperation seem to deteriorate as the push and pull of money forces people to take stands they probably wouldn't take in better times. Several of our colleagues theorize that high net-worth couples tend to divorce more when the economy is good, and they ride out the recessions. Lower-income couples, those with less to lose, are more likely to go ahead and divorce when the economy is bad.

The more money couples have, the more planning they seem to do for divorce. We've had many clients come in before they decide to divorce, in hopes that they can get their financial affairs in order before they file. Usually they intend to file within a couple of months, or in a specific time frame. Waiting until after the end-of-the-year holidays is popular, and throughout the state the first quarter of the year — January through March — is the time when the greatest number of divorce filings happens.

Decide whether you will use traditional litigation or collaborative law as early in the process as possible.

No doubt about it, battling all the way to the courthouse in a divorce can cause irreparable harm to the entire family, kids included. It can leave a mark that will not go away over time. Some cases have to be litigated for the parties to feel they got their day in court and be able to move on. Others are ripe for the collaborative law process.

We will discuss the mechanics of collaborative law in more detail later in this book, but suffice it to say that you should consider the pros and cons of using collaborative law instead of litigation in your divorce. You can decide what kind of divorce you will have. Will it be the divorce from hell or do you want your children to look back on this time and think that mommy and daddy helped them get through a difficult time?

CHAPTER 3

What Kind of Divorce Will This Be?

IMMEDIATELY AFTER THE DECISION to divorce is made, think about the type of divorce you want. Will the two of you walk away from the process thinking pleasant thoughts about each other, or will you throw make-believe daggers at each other for decades to come? Do you have children to consider? How do you want them to recall this time? Remember that you are halfway responsible for the tone and tenor of your dissolution. If you plan to contest the terms of your divorce, do it in a sane and sensible manner.

An uncontested divorce means that people who agree on very little in a marriage — to the point of pulling the plug on the whole thing — will come together and agree on everything involved in saying goodbye. Many divorces start out cordial enough. Then he or she talks to friends. Ego, pride, jealousy, rage and resentment intermingle with substantive property issues. Someone says something, and that earlier spirit of agreement is destroyed. An uncontested divorce suddenly becomes both contested and expensive.

If you want to keep conflict to a minimum, restrain yourself. Keep your mouth shut and stick to the business of divorce. Many agreements that are perfectly fair to both parties collapse after one spouse says something that offends the other before the papers are executed. There are good reasons to nullify agreements, but pride and ego are not among them.

If your spouse offers to keep things low-key and believes the two of you should hire just one attorney to "paper" the divorce, be wary. An attorney can represent only one party in a divorce. That attorney may stand in court with you, but he or she is protecting the interests of one client, and the other party's rights can be greatly affected by the terms of any settlement agreement entered into between the parties.

If your spouse insists on having just one attorney between the two of you, make sure the attorney is representing you. Without that protection, prepare yourself for a disaster that could affect you for the rest of your life.

Can Your Spouse Remain a Friend?

How important is it for you to remain on speaking terms with your soon-to-be ex-spouse? In consultation with an attorney, decide what that friendship is worth. How much are you willing to concede to keep the other side happy?

At a time like this, when you are most vulnerable, the steady hand of an emotionally disinterested party who is experienced at handling divorce matters may keep you from making the mistake of a lifetime.

If you want to dissolve your marriage while still protecting yourself, have a matrimonial law expert assess your situation, inform you of your rights and advise you about various scenarios that might save you trouble in the long run.

There often comes a time in many divorces when communication breaks down and progress grinds to a halt. This is when a divorce may become contested and difficult. Often this point comes when you least expect it, in the midst of negotiations that are meant to end the struggle but just create more emotion and heat.

To ready yourself, remember that your spouse is looking out for himself or herself, if just for the duration of the divorce. This person wants to keep assets that you may need to pay bills. This may sound cutthroat, but it is true. Of course, you may need to temper that feeling if young children are involved. After all, your spouse will be your child's parent for the rest of his or her life and you will be forever bound together by that child.

Gain Access to Information

Often married couples include what you might call a "documented" spouse and an "undocumented" one. The documented spouse usually makes most of the money, pays the bills and maintains the records. The undocumented spouse has little to do with family finances. That spouse is at a distinct disadvantage at the beginning of a divorce case. If you are the undocumented spouse, you will want to gain access to important information and become well documented.

Never allow your spouse to control the documents. Think of yourself as an information magnet in the early days of your divorce. Information can make or break your case at trial. Insist on being a partner in the process of paying bills. It is much easier to gather the financial information while the marriage is working than after the divorce is filed and everyone becomes suspicious of each other.

The most relevant items you must gather include three to five years of the following:

- Personal and corporate tax returns
- Checking, savings and money market account statements
- Investment account statements
- Stock and bond certificates
- Financial statements
- Mortgage papers
- Credit card information
- Information on debts and other liabilities
- Long-distance telephone bills
- Cellular telephone bills
- Medical records
- Health insurance policies
- Life insurance policies
- Any evidence that establishes fault by the other side

Put this information away for safekeeping. It may or may not be pertinent if used at trial or in settlement negotiations. But you want the opportunity to make that decision by having it available. Your attorney should prompt you for any other information you might need for your case.

Obtaining this information does not assure you of winning most of the marital assets in a divorce. The facts of your case will dictate how the assets will be divided. But the information should be available to you for a variety of reasons, such as your

spouse's death or illness. With your family's financial information in hand, you can exert more control and know what is at
stake.

Bank account records reveal crucial information. Often they
contain facts and figures known by only one of the marriage
partners. For example, most employed people get paid twice
a month, so the account would include deposits to a checking
account, customarily, on the first and 15th day of each month.
What if your spouse claims a monthly income of $10,000 but
you discover that he or she deposits $25,000 into the check-
ing account each month? This may indicate large commissions,
bonuses or other money your spouse has received from an
unknown source. You need to know the source of that income.
It could make a huge difference in the division of assets or the
amount of child support your spouse might be ordered to pay.

Asset tracing is a delicate skill and one we will deal with in
greater detail in a later chapter. Information obtained through
investigation can become devastatingly effective pieces of evidence. Long-distance and cellular telephone records are great
examples. You can establish an illicit relationship with page
after page of cellular calls to a certain number.

The opposing lawyer may request both personal and business cellular phone and long-distance records for the past three
to five years. If a spouse has been hiding these calls behind
business accounts, the information will prove valuable and the
guilty spouse could settle the case to keep an employer from
finding out how he or she has been spending company time and
money.

Too often, people operate on a hunch, suspecting something without being able to prove it. Proof is the divider between

whether your information is effective or not. If you can't prove it, don't bring it up. Presenting potentially damaging information without solid proof just makes you look vindictive and deceitful. The decision whether to present certain evidence is not an easy one. This decision has to be made in the context of the overall strategy of your case.

Seven Simple Steps to Prepare for Divorce

Divorcing parties often get all the way through the process without having discussed with their attorneys what personal items they want and whether they can actually afford to pay for the marital residence they cannot live without. If you see a divorce coming in your life, batten down the financial hatches. Here's what divorce lawyers and financial planners suggest at the start:

1. Prepare a list of the family's assets and liabilities. Know where to find financial documents and make copies.
2. Start saving money in your own separate bank account, so you'll have cash to pay bills. You will have to disclose these funds, but at least you will have immediate access to them.
3. Decide which assets you would like to keep and which you are willing to give up.
4. Don't expect the same lifestyle you enjoyed when you were married. Divorce can be financially devastating to both partners.
5. Apply for credit in your own name so you can start building an individual credit history.

6. Know the divorce laws. Texas is a community property state. The court must decide what constitutes your community property and divide those assets. Depending on your case, a court may not divide assets equally.

7. Gather the documents and proof necessary to prove your separate property claims.

Think Strategically

Our approach to divorce is like our view of world events. Our policy could be summed up as peace through strength. Another way to put it is that we should never let our enemies see us sweat. Recognize that your spouse is the opposition. Don't show your weaknesses while gathering information.

Hostilities typically begin with informal negotiations. Separate your emotions from the practical objective of reaching a settlement on your terms. Use these negotiations to find out what the opposition wants, but don't let on that the ragged beige chair in the living room is still your most prized possession. Handle things as if the case will wind up in trial. If it settles, you are ahead of the game.

If your own emotions are lethal, those of your friends and family can be nuclear. Many divorces start in a sane manner. Then family members, buddies and girlfriends begin to talk about what is right, how much you could get, how far you could push and what your other friends have gotten.

Be realistic about the facts of your case. Realize that evidence is essential and that witnesses are needed to substantiate your claims in court. Both are necessary to a successful financial divorce.

CHAPTER 4

WITH OR WITHOUT AN ATTORNEY

DECIDING HOW HARD TO PUSH and who to trust are important decisions in a divorce. So much is riding on the outcome that you want to structure your divorce correctly and choose the best way to achieve your goals. A wise partner of ours once said that a divorce is the largest business deal most of us will ever undertake. Mess this one up and you will have a difficult time maintaining your lifestyle for the foreseeable future.

The standard for divorce cases in Texas is two warring parties, two attorneys and a judge or jury. But there are alternatives to the litigation model, some more productive than others.

Representing Yourself

Do-it-yourself divorces are on the rise all over the country. Cities that track the number of people who file pro se (Latin for "in one's own behalf") indicate that as many as one-half of their divorce, child custody and abuse cases include at least one party without a lawyer. In some places, that's a doubling of the number of people acting as their own attorney over the past decade. In Texas, as in other jurisdictions, you have the right to represent yourself in court. Some people feel they can't afford an attorney. Others believe their cases are so simple that they don't need an attorney. But a growing segment of the do-it-yourself crowd include people who've surfed the myriad of divorce websites on the Internet and feel they can handle their own affairs.

This category of pro se litigant brings more complex cases to court, according to mediator Jeff Coen, a former family court judge. "Today, we find a larger percentage of our pro se litigants who distrust or dislike lawyers or won't hire lawyers because they want the control of doing it themselves. So the cases are not based on being simple or easy. They've not only risen in volume, but in complexity and the amount of time the courts must provide them."

Lawyers and judges are perplexed by this trend. Pro se litigants often don't know the rules of court and can't fill out the forms correctly. They may not know how to address the judge or understand the need for evidence in a case. If they are awarded property, they don't know how to take possession of it. The judge will hold them to the standards expected of a lawyer. They often fail to prove that certain assets are separate property, which may result in a finding that those assets are community property and can be awarded to the other spouse.

In some of Texas' urban counties, though, the courts have initiated efforts to facilitate pro se representation. "We started a pro se docket where litigants could bring their paperwork ahead of time to get approval," says Coen. "They actually had their own day to prove up cases and receive instruction from judges and attorneys."

Some of these same legal professionals host forums to teach pro se litigants how to handle themselves in court and where to get help if they need it. But having a confused litigant is not the most dangerous aspect of pro se representation.

Making a mistake at this important juncture can adversely affect your future. In cases that are truly uncontested, involving no children or property, representing yourself may be a viable alternative. This would be analogous to the home do-it-your-selfer attempting to retile a bathroom and botching the job. You may regret your decision to tackle this project, but it's unlikely to destroy your home.

If you have children, extensive amounts of property or other complex arrangements between you and your spouse, pro se representation is more like performing surgery on yourself. It's deadly serious, with the possibility of spoiling the future.

If you plan to represent yourself, locate and attend a pro se divorce clinic before going to court. Legal services organizations and men's and women's rights groups generally run these clinics. Often a family law attorney stands by at the clinic to guide you through the process, teach you how to prepare the necessary documents and answer your questions. You, however, will appear by yourself at the final hearing.

Sharing One Attorney

Perhaps the only method less certain than handling your own divorce is to use one attorney to represent both parties. As discussed earlier, one attorney cannot represent the interests of two clients in the same divorce. But it happens over and over again that the most streetwise spouse tries to convince the less experienced spouse that their futures can be secured by using the "couple's" attorney.

A prime example is the client who agreed with her husband to keep their divorce inexpensive and civil. She worked out the property division with the husband, who was an older man and an experienced businessperson. When the couple agreed on the settlement, they submitted it to his company attorney to paper the divorce.

Among the information the husband provided the attorney was a valuation of his business along with details of their bank accounts and investments. The woman trusted the attorney, who had been a guest in their home many times. Everyone behaved cooperatively until she discovered a bank account her husband and the attorney failed to disclose. She became more suspicious when her husband provided the business valuation and it came back very low. Only then did the woman hire her own attorney, who immediately deduced that the man was trying to cheat his wife out of several hundred thousand dollars. Luckily, the divorce was not final and the new attorney rectified the situation.

Can you trust your soon-to-be ex-spouse to lay out all the facts before you? And can you rely on an attorney you didn't hire? Under Texas law, that attorney has no obligation to serve your interests.

The Importance of a Specialist

Locating an attorney who connects with your personality and has enough experience to handle your case is essential. It's ironic that many people put less time and effort into the purchase of legal services than they do into buying a pair of new shoes.

We live in a consumer society, and you must look at legal services as a consumer product that you should purchase wisely. Hire the services of a matrimonial law expert who is prepared to handle your case. The law has become very specialized over the past few decades and most attorneys now concentrate in one or two practice areas.

The Texas Board of Legal Specialization recognizes those attorneys in the state who spend most of their working life on a specific practice area. An attorney who is board certified in family law by the Texas Board of Legal Specialization spends the majority of his time on divorces, child custody and other family law-related matters.

Whatever your need, there is an attorney who can help you. More than one million attorneys practice in the United States, more than 70,000 of them in Texas alone. If you have friends who are divorced, begin your search by asking them for recommendations. You may know an attorney who practices in a field other than matrimonial law. Ask that attorney to refer you to a good family lawyer.

Your local bar association may offer a referral service. Marriage counselors and therapists, accountants, financial planners, business managers and clergymen often know family lawyers with outstanding reputations and good track records.

From these sources, you can also find out if the strengths of certain attorneys meet your needs. For instance, if you have a business, large assets or other complex property issues, you need to hire a firm with the capabilities and staff to manage a large asset case. The goal of any good family lawyer is settlement. But if you realistically believe your case may end up in court, make sure your attorney is a skilled and effective trial lawyer.

Even if you find an attorney with the best possible reputation, don't stop there. You are still operating on the opinions of others. You want a person you will enjoy working with over the months it can take to finalize a divorce.

Initial Interviews

There may be many attorneys in your town with the legal ability to do the job. Isolate at least two of them and schedule initial interviews. What you're looking for is the most qualified attorney who best suits your personality. You could be working in close proximity with this person for a year or more. Life is too short to spend that time with someone you personally dislike.

A short interview with each of the qualified candidates will tell you which attorney best suits you. Each attorney will want to discuss the basic history of the marriage and the issues involved in the divorce. Be as candid as possible, letting the attorney know your good points and your faults. Lawyers are under an ethical obligation not to disclose the information you provide, unless you consent to the disclosure. The following items are very helpful for the lawyer to know at the initial meeting:

- Length of the marriage
- Names and ages of children and any special needs
- Fault of either spouse
- Each party's relationship with the children and child care responsibilities
- Income of each party
- Work history of each party
- Summary of assets and debts

The lawyer may ask you to prepare a detailed timeline and summary of the marital history after the initial interview. He or she needs to know each and every issue your spouse could bring up during the case. It is impossible for the attorney to correctly evaluate your case unless you present him or her with all the facts on both sides.

Questions to Ask Your Attorney

"Do you charge for the initial interview?"

Most matrimonial lawyers charge for the initial visit, while a few offer a free consultation. The fee charged is typically the hourly rate of the attorney and can range from $150 to several hundred dollars. In most cases, if you hire the attorney at the initial visit, the interview charge is paid from the retainer.

The initial interview creates a conflict situation for the lawyer. Once an attorney meets with one spouse and hears the marital history, he or she cannot represent the other spouse.

"How do you charge for your services?"

Most matrimonial lawyers bill on an hourly basis for work performed by the lawyers and paralegals. Become a smart consumer of legal services and choose the attorney who can meet your expectations at a price you can afford. Expect to be billed each time you meet with the lawyer, call him or her on the telephone or the office staff works on your case. You should understand how the lawyer bills. If you don't understand billing procedures, ask questions.

You wouldn't purchase an item from a department store without knowing the purchase price or allow the plumber to bill you whatever amount comes to mind. Make certain your lawyer is only charging you for time spent on your case.

"Do I sign a fee agreement?"

Most lawyers execute a written fee agreement when you make a hiring decision. Review the agreement and understand how you will be billed and what other expenses you are obligated to pay. Determine the initial retainer and when it must be paid. A retainer is an advance payment for time and expenses and the lawyer typically bills against this retainer each month for work performed on your behalf.

These days, most lawyers refund unused retainers. For example, a client may initially sign a fee agreement providing a $10,000 retainer to the attorney. That attorney may do $7,000 worth of legal work on the case, but then the parties decide to reconcile, the case is finalized or the client comes to the conclusion that this attorney is not the right one for this case. The remaining $3,000 is handled according to the agreement, and usually that means the client receives a refund.

Because the initial retainer may not be enough for the complete divorce, the fee agreement should also address supplemental retainers throughout the case. If it is a large-asset case or is hotly litigated, the client may be required to supplement the retainer several times during the process.

The agreement should specify what expenses a client is obligated to pay, such as long-distance charges, subpoena fees and photocopy and fax charges. The fee agreement may also address the possibility that one spouse is required by the court to pay the other's legal fees and how that payment would be applied.

Some lawyers offer to handle divorces for a flat fee payment, but it's difficult for an attorney to pinpoint exactly how much a case will cost at the outset. How the client conducts himself or herself, plus the actions of the other spouse, the opposing attorney or others involved in the case affect the cost.

The tremendous expense involved in litigating a divorce with many financial and emotional components may be shocking. Fees in a divorce handled on an hourly basis can range from several thousand dollars to a hundred thousand dollars or more, depending on the assets, issues and personalities involved.

"Who is my contact in the firm?"

During the initial interview, determine which attorneys and staff members will work on your case. Some firms consist of one lawyer, a paralegal and a receptionist, so the contact points are obvious.

At this writing, our firm is the largest in the Southwest that handles exclusively family law cases. We have more than 20 lawyers in four offices, plus paralegals, secretaries and other professionals. It is helpful for the client to have more than one point of contact within our firm. If a client calls and the lawyer with primary responsibility for that case is in a conference or is out of the office, other members of the firm can address emergencies until the primary attorney returns.

Many large-asset cases require the attention of two or more lawyers. For example, one lawyer may concentrate on the facts of the marriage and the witnesses to those facts while another lawyer works specifically on assets and business issues related to the case. It is enough for one attorney to know the history of a 20-year marriage with three children and a spouse with an addiction problem. Another attorney may concentrate on the financial terms, conditions and history of a successful multimillion-dollar business, along with the details of the purchase and acquisition of all assets and debts of the marriage.

If your case involves significant assets, debts or other complications, make certain the lawyer you hire has the necessary experience and time to prepare your case. You know everything about your case because you have been living it. Your attorney is probably very interested in the facts of your case, but you must bring the lawyer up to speed so that he or she may either negotiate a settlement or try the case, explaining all the details to the judge or jury.

"Do you send out monthly statements?"

Monitor the charges incurred in your case on a regular basis. Lawyers and staff members must compile a lot of information to prepare your case for trial. Even if you are not talking to the lawyer on a regular basis, work is probably being done on your behalf.

Use your lawyer's time wisely. If you call the lawyer daily and use the law firm as an emotional counseling service, your bill will increase dramatically. At most firms, attorneys and paralegals record their time each day. Monthly statements inform the client about the billing charges incurred and the work that generated those charges. We ask clients to review our monthly statements and call with any questions.

"How long will my case take?"

A divorce that settles is generally resolved faster than one that is litigated. A case that goes to trial could take a year to 18 months from start to finish. Some cases take longer than two years to resolve due to intricacies, delays and obstructions. If you are headed toward litigation, count on a year or more of preparation and delay until you have your divorce. Delays are due to the large number of divorce cases in the court system as well as the effort required to determine the assets and other issues involved.

If your spouse fails to provide financial records, you may have to subpoena those records or get a court order to obtain them. In these instances, your case will take longer to resolve than if both sides put all the information on the table. If you must provide audits and detailed financial examinations of the assets and values of the businesses involved, take into account the scheduling and availability of other professionals.

If you, your spouse or his or her lawyer decide to battle every facet of the case, your divorce will take longer and become a great deal more expensive. Many cases start out as litigated matters while tempers and emotions run high. But time and mounting fees sometimes calm those emotions and allow the parties to settle.

We try to determine the assets, debts and other significant issues involved and proceed down the path of settlement in each case. Some cases, though, must litigate because the other side won't allow them to settle. Sometimes having the judge make a ruling resolves the case more quickly and reasonably than expecting the parties to resolve their differences themselves.

"What do you expect of me?"

Get a sense of how much cooperation the lawyer expects from you. We generally give homework to each client. This homework usually involves the client obtaining or developing information to help us fully understand the case. Fee agreements often explain that the client's cooperation is critical. Many firms reserve the right to withdraw from a case if the client will not help the lawyer obtain information only available to the client or if he or she is not honest with the lawyer. While it's not necessary to communicate with the lawyer every day, it is in your best interest to provide the requested information in a timely fashion. If the lawyer calls to schedule an appointment or obtain additional information, return the call as soon as possible. You should care about the outcome of your divorce case at least as much as your attorney.

Dedicate a certain amount of time on a regular basis to helping your lawyer prepare. In our experience, a client who is thoroughly involved in the preparation and details of the case is more informed and is always happier with the end result.

Guarantees vs. Experience

No attorney can guarantee a certain outcome in your divorce case, but an experienced family law specialist can give you a range of possibilities to expect. A good attorney can evaluate your case and let you know how he or she believes a judge or jury will react to your evidence.

"If you can divorce in Texas without bloodletting the family, then do it....
All good lawyers can resolve a case with a settlement through some type of mediation. Find a lawyer who can do this. It's a much better option than pulling out the six-shooters to get it done...."

Ike Vanden Eykel
"When Dallas Couples Decide to Split,
New Divorce Methods Help Them Keep it Together"
D Magazine

CHAPTER 5

COLLABORATIVE LAW

DURING THE 1990s, family law experts frustrated with the destructive nature of divorce litigation developed a new approach known as collaborative law. This was a radical departure from the more adversarial way of dissolving families.

A Paradigm Shift in Family Law

Collaborative law is often compared with mediation, the other important form of alternative dispute resolution. But while mediation is a dispute resolution method used in conjunction with litigation, collaborative law represents a complete paradigm shift in the way divorcing people relate to each other and attorneys relate to the parties.

As practiced in Texas, collaborative law involves the two divorcing parties and their attorneys meeting face to face from the beginning of the case in a series of settlement sessions working toward agreement on all the issues involved in a divorce.

The goal is to reduce the level of hostility and produce a settlement that maximizes assets and relationships. Divorcing people who want to continue relationships with their ex-spouses are most likely to use collaborative law. This includes couples with children, those who own or operate a family business, people who share the same workplace and those who have the same large group of friends and don't want to lose any of them in the divorce.

"Too often, one of the major casualties of divorce is a person's dignity," says our partner, Kevin Fuller, whose practice includes collaborative law as well as litigated divorces. "When you choose to litigate your divorce, you often have to lay your most private facts out in a public forum. Collaborative law is especially useful to people who want to resolve disputes — from the custody of children to very large property cases — with their personal and financial dignity intact."

This process is strictly voluntary, although some Texas judges are beginning to recommend that certain families consider it. Ideally, collaborative law participants never see the inside of a courtroom. The sessions take place in law firm conference rooms, for the most part, and are kept informal and low stress. Most collaborative law divorces are settled in a series of six two-hour sessions over several weeks.

If Settlement Fails, Attorneys Must Withdraw

The unique agreements about the conduct and structure of negotiations the parties and their attorneys make at the outset distinguish collaborative law from mediation and litigation. If the case does not settle and litigation becomes necessary, both collaborative lawyers must withdraw from the case. Clients must hire other trial attorneys if they want to litigate the divorce. Although most collaborative attorneys also litigate divorces on occasion, they cannot wear both hats in the same case. This makes sense because the collaborative process requires that everyone feel comfortable discussing the facts of the case. Collaborative law participants certainly wouldn't feel safe sharing personal information with an attorney on the other side who could wind up deposing or cross-examining them in court.

Attorneys in litigated divorces are sometimes accused of sabotaging settlements so that negotiations fail and the attorneys can justify taking a case to court. Attorney fees in these contentious cases can be significant. The poison pill feature of collaborative law (where attorneys must withdraw if they can't settle) removes any incentive attorneys might have to stretch out the divorce and increase fees.

Collaborative law has the potential to save money in the short term. Its sensible approach to divorce has an even greater potential to set divorcing couples on a long-term path to financial security.

Dallas collaborative family lawyer Janet Brumley, author of *Divorce Without Disaster: Collaborative Law in Texas*, writes, "a survey in *American Lawyer* magazine estimates that the average attorney fees in a collaborative law case are about one-third the amount of a litigated divorce."

Many collaborative lawyers practice in groups of independent, unaffiliated legal professionals, because two attorneys trained in collaborative law do the best job handling collaborative cases. Many of these practice groups utilize a team approach, bringing in family therapists, financial planners, CPAs, estate planners and other professionals to organize the finances of the parties and help them begin their new lives.

The result, Brumley writes in *Divorce Without Disaster*, is as follows:

> *"Money is only one thing you save. Pursuing divorce collaboratively can save you everything—time, your children's self-esteem, friendships, privacy, assets and whatever relationship you have left with your spouse."*

Locate a Collaborative Lawyer

Collaborative law practice groups operate in most Texas urban areas. You are less likely to find a local group if you live in a small town or rural area of the state. If you are interested in exploring the possibility of a collaborative law divorce, check out the following websites for to find a collaboratively trained family attorney in your area:

Collaborative Law Institute of Texas
www.collablawtexas.com
International Academy of Collaborative Professionals
www.collabgroup.com

A few lawyers who handle cases collaboratively are not members of practice groups, so you should ask if a certain attorney handles collaborative cases.

HE SAID SHE SAID: A More Humane Method

<u>He said</u> they were married about five years too long. He couldn't remember the last time he felt alive and looked forward to coming home at night. Most evenings, he used any excuse to stay late at work and avoid dinner with a wife who didn't hear how his day went and didn't seem to care.

The first 10 years of their marriage they were young and in love, tackling the milestones in life with a remarkable ease that made others envious. When they made investments, the payoffs were always substantial. In some ways, especially financial, they led charmed lives. He could hardly remember a time when they really fought or disagreed on anything. They just seemed like the perfect couple to all of their friends and family.

But the ease with which they approached life was deceiving and they began to drift apart. He missed the days when she used to dote over him.

Without ever arguing or screaming at each other, he decided to take his life back. It would be a messy divorce, not because of any animosity between them but because of their latest financial venture. They invested in a start-up company, a fragile newcomer that could easily be destroyed by shaky ownership.

Concern for their two children, the relationship with his wife and the health of the new company drove him to consult a colleague who recently split from his wife. The colleague suggested an attorney who practices mostly in the new area of collaborative law, and the next day he called the attorney and set up an appointment. He was nervous, not sure he was making the best decision, but for his own happiness he had to explore this option.

Before they had children, a house and two demanding careers, he and his wife were the best of friends. He tried countless attempts to rekindle this love and friendship. But she didn't seem to want him near her and he could not imagine continuing. When the attorney questioned him about his priorities, he listed his children, his happiness, their friendship and his new business venture as being most important.

Collaborative law was designed to keep the divorce out of litigation and help him preserve the important matters, both emotionally and financially. He eagerly took brochures and other information on this method and would talk to her about it.

She said she could remember the crazy and unpredictable things he would do in the early years. Since the children were born, she noticed his spark and enthusiasm for life melting away.

She used to pamper him and take care of his every need when they were first married. She always had strong maternal feelings and worked hard to make him happy. When she said it was time they start a family, he stalled until she agreed that they would have just one child.

He wasn't as happy as she wanted him to be about their young son, but he seemed to be getting accustomed to it. Without any thought or planning, nine months later, she discovered she was pregnant again. He wasn't thrilled with the idea, but there wasn't anything they could do about it now. When their daughter was born, she could not believe how much time and energy two small children consumed.

Gradually he seemed more and more uncomfortable at home because he never talked about his job and preferred to spend his free time watching TV or playing games on the computer.

She knew they were drifting apart and he was unhappy, but when he came home talking about a divorce, she was blindsided. Everything she had ever dreamed about was slipping away. She suggested marriage counseling, but he said that even counseling could not heal his feeling of just wanting to be alone. All she could do was nod as he explained how they could dissolve the marriage without the messiness they had seen in other divorces.

The result was a collaborative law divorce designed to save their friendship, protect their children from the heartache of a drawn-out ordeal and allow them to retain their considerable assets. Once she selected a collaborative law attorney, her attorney called his attorney and they arranged a time for their first joint session.

They met at her attorney's office. He knew she was nervous and unsure of the process, so he tried to give her as much control of the session as possible. The meeting started with a short introduction and a reading of the collaborative law participation agreement. After the attorneys finished reading, they asked for any general questions on the process itself. The attorneys explained that the process would take at least 60 days, since the state of Texas requires that a divorce petition be on file for that long before it can be finalized. But many divorces take longer and this is no one's fault. Everyone agreed that they would work one session at a time until everything was resolved and the final decree was ready to be signed in court.

They established that the purpose of the sessions was to determine the best arrangement for their children, divide property and possibly designate alimony. The attorneys made it clear that hashing out marital disagreements or airing the other spouse's dirty laundry was usually not productive during the sessions. Both attorneys suggested they have a mental health professional present in the meetings and that the couple seek therapy to work through any unresolved issues before going any farther with the process. Both agreed and they moved on to the goals they hoped to accomplish with collaborative law.

They worked through several sessions as well as meeting regularly with the family therapist. Though they kept things civilized, it was still painful. During the sessions, they decided that she would have primary possession of the children and each of them would have specified days with the kids. They agreed that he would retain ownership in the new company and she would get their home. He kept his retirement accounts and agreed to pay her substantial maintenance payments over five years.

At several points in the negotiations, emotions ran high. When he asked to have the children half the summer, she broke down and stormed out of the session. When they began to talk about their home, she again began sobbing, but regained her composure. The weekend after they finalized an agreement about visitation, he got confused and brought the children home late on Sunday night. She was upset, but they worked through it. He gave her as much latitude as possible, since his attorney told him that she was not as far along in the process of disengagement as he was and he needed to be understanding.

The final session turned into their longest one. They finalized the house agreement, ownership of the new business interest and the custody, possession and child support agreements. Without much conflict they divvied up the rest of the household items and the little debt they accumulated as a couple. With the final session winding down, neither of them could believe they were still talking to one another right before the divorce was to be final.

CHAPTER 6

SAVE MONEY ON LEGAL FEES

DODEE CROCKETT HAS a special function when she consults with a client facing a divorce. As an advisor to high-net-worth individuals in Dallas, her main job is to help her clients establish money goals and implement strategies to achieve them. In a divorce, she puts down the sword and shield of a wealth warrior and becomes the trusted translator of legalese.

Educate Yourself

"Some attorneys are very good at telling clients the what, where and how," says the longtime Merrill Lynch advisor. "Only the very best attorneys tell people why they are doing something. You may need someone else involved who can fill in the communication gaps, talking to the client about why he or she is giving a deposition or requesting a hearing."

In a deposition, your attorney may feel that learning the whereabouts of certain assets is worth the expense of deposing your spouse. You may already know where those assets are located and you just neglected to tell your attorney. You may not fully understand the reason for the deposition, but believe it is standard procedure in such a case. You may not know you are about to incur an expense to get information you already have.

If your attorney fails to discuss his or her reasoning for a certain action, bring up the subject yourself.

"Why are we deposing my ex?" may seem like a dumb question, but asking it may help you avoid an expensive mistake. Such questions also educate you about this process, and education can help you through the process without breaking the bank.

Contingency Fees

The disciplinary rules of the State Bar of Texas state that contingent fee arrangements in family law cases are rarely justified.

Making legal fees in divorce cases contingent on recovery presents a unique set of problems because of the human relationships involved and the nature of the proceedings. Don't confuse the billing practices of divorce lawyers with advertisements you see on television for personal injury attorneys who promise that you don't have to pay "unless we collect." When that payday comes, the attorney takes from one-third to one-half of the award or settlement plus costs, and the client receives the remainder.

The rule makers in Texas believe that contingent fees in a divorce case can create a conflict of interest between the lawyer and the client, with the attorney possibly pressuring the client to accept an inadequate settlement so he or she can get paid. There is also the question of valuing non-cash assets so the attorney can get his cut. In some family law matters, such as child custody, contingent fee arrangements are unworkable because there is no property to fund a fee.

10 Effective Strategies for Controlling Legal Fees

Remember that the meter is running each time some work must be done on your case. Take responsibility for keeping legal fees under control by adhering to the following strategies:

1. Let your attorney know from the start that money is an issue.

2. Be aware that each time you meet with your attorney, talk on the telephone to the attorney or staff or they work on your behalf, it costs you money.

3. Don't use your attorney or the staff as a counseling service. This can be very expensive.

4. Help your attorney collect financial information, track down documents and do other work he or she would have to pay someone to do.

5. Each time during the divorce that you do anything designed to keep your fees down, tell your attorney that is what you are doing. A friendly reminder never hurts.

6. Distinguish a real emergency from the panic of divorce. Emergency calls to your attorney after hours and on weekends can cost you a lot of money.

7. Don't encourage (or allow) your attorney to secure an asset that is worth less than the cost of acquiring it.

8. Let your attorney know which assets are important to you and which ones are not. Fighting on too many fronts can be expensive.

9. If you feel you can settle certain sticky issues on your own, such as custody of your children or who should run a family business, do so with your attorney's advice.

10. Never tell your attorney to "do whatever it takes." This is the same as saying you don't care how much it costs.

CHAPTER 7

WORK TOWARD SETTLEMENT

THE UNEQUAL DIVORCE SETTLEMENT is a compelling feature of American cultural lore. It's somehow fashionable to assert that you "got taken" in the divorce and many times we have heard both sides in a divorce claim they got the short end of the deal. Studies show that people feel better about their divorce when they take an active part in a settlement of the case, rather than going to court and having a judge or jury decide what happens. That's why we believe settlements in which both sides give some and take some are preferable to almost any court verdict.

What Is Fair?

Fairness does not always mean an equal distribution of assets. Since Texas is a community property state, both parties normally own assets acquired during the marriage on an equal basis. But the law does not say the community assets in a divorce must be divided equally. If the parties cannot agree on a property division, the court can divide the community property, taking under consideration a variety of factors. The following are among the most important factors judges often consider:

- Length of the marriage
- The ages, occupations, health and employability of the parties, and their ability to be trained
- Earning capacity of the parties
- Diminished earning capacity because of years spent caring for children
- Which spouse has custody of children
- Size of the parties' separate estates
- Prospects for each party to acquire additional capital, assets or income in the future
- Fault of the parties in the marriage breakup

With these factors in mind, few people are absolutely equal in a judge's eyes. If the couple has been married for many years, they are near retirement and the wife has never worked outside the home, they have no assets maturing in the future and the man has been having an affair, the wife might get more assets.

Major Financial Blunders

An experienced family lawyer, sometimes with the help of a valuation expert, will provide you with information to help you determine what the assets of your marriage are worth.

Only you can decide where you draw the line and which assets are worth a fight. On countless occasions, we have seen divorcing people make the following major financial blunders:

- Incorrectly valuing a closely held business
- Failing to consider the tax effect of certain assets
- Being unaware that retirement accounts, stock options, deferred compensation plans and accrued bonuses can be divided between the parties
- Failing to consider the debts in a marriage

There are many smaller blunders made by clients and their attorneys each day. For instance, most people forget that such assets as frequent flyer miles or the points you receive from using certain credit cards have value. They overlook tax prepayments, tax loss carry forwards and employee stock options or fail to realize when one party prepays a debt from community funds on an asset that is separate property.

Most Cases Settle

Let us emphasize once again that it is in your best interest, in almost all cases, to work out an amicable division of personal property instead of having a judge do it. You know what you want and can go into more detail about it. A judge doesn't really want to divide your personal property and often resents having to spend valuable time on this exercise. He or she will divide the property quickly, as part of the resolution of the entire case, and is unaware of any sentimental attachments you have to specific items unless you make them known. Only you really care that you are fond of the armoire or that only you watched the big-screen television.

Often a judge will draw a line somewhere down the list of property. It could be an even split, but that's not guaranteed.

Even if you have to go to court over more significant issues, you can divide the personal property prior to trial and eliminate some issues that otherwise would be submitted to the judge.

Sometimes a specific piece of personal property takes on a meaning that far outweighs its value. In one case, child custody was the issue that brought the parties into court. With that issue resolved, all that remained was possession of a vintage automobile that was very special to the man. Because the car was so special to him, the woman fought him over it for months. Without the battle over this car, the parents and children could have begun to heal from the divorce months earlier.

The Importance of Mediation

Mediation has affected more people than any other feature of family law in the past quarter century. Although mediation began in California, it is used most extensively in Texas to expedite the settlement of cases in family court.

Moving the divorce away from the courthouse and into the mediator's office can often reduce the adversarial tension inherent in the process. The job of a divorce lawyer in court is to win for the client. The job of a mediator is to negotiate the best deal possible by crafting an agreement that will hold up over time.

The most productive mediations are those presided over by a domestic relations attorney. The basic philosophy of divorce mediation is that even two people who despise each other can reach an accord if a neutral third party, trained in the intricacies of negotiation, guides them through it. A divorce mediator asks incisive questions, cuts through anger and hurt and facilitates rational decision-making that can lead to a successful divorce.

"No matter how contentious a divorce may be, the objective of every case is to settle in the most advantageious way possible, although Koons Fuller attorneys are all prepared to take a case to the courthouse. It's just that over time, the attorneys of this firm have found that the 'scorched earth' policy which once characterized divorce only occasionally meets a client's needs and goals."

Society Life Magazine
April 2009

Dallas mediator R.B. Pool was a family lawyer for 15 years before he started handling mediations after Texas amended the Family Code in 1987. From just a handful of cases the first year, Pool has seen the number of mediations "spread like wildfire all over Texas."

Today, he insists, "Virtually every court in the state will send you to mediation before they give you two or three days of trial time. About 85% of all cases that go to mediation settle, so this has lightened the courts' caseload where mediation is required or highly recommended."

Those early mediation participants were the couples going through friendly divorces, but who needed a boost to bring them to closure. Today, he says, even highly adversarial parties embrace this settlement method. "Mediators attempt to determine what's going to happen at the courthouse, how their particular judge might rule and how much money it will cost to get there.

"In mediation," Pool explains, "you can forge your own destiny. But at the courthouse, you are absolutely without control. The judge has the final say. If two people work for 30 years to build something together, it's tough to let a third party divide it."

The actual structure of the mediation proceedings varies according to the mediator. Some mediators believe that placing two people face to face in a room is the best way to forge an agreement.

In some cases, the actual mediation process begins with the parties and their representatives meeting for a few minutes in the same room. Here the mediator lays out the ground rules.

Then the parties are separated and the mediator shuttles from room to room highlighting points of agreement and helping the parties think of creative ways to resolve the case. Pool, like many other mediators, doesn't believe his job is to "force something down someone's throat. My primary purpose is to see if there is some common ground on which everyone is willing to perch. They won't necessarily like it, but they must be willing to look at an educated alternative to going to trial."

Most mediation sessions last an entire day and the parties may elect to stay in session until settlement is reached. The best mediators effectively use the time to reach common goals.

The Benefits Are Significant

A middle-class couple that decides to do battle can rack up legal expenses in the six-figure range and take an entire presidential administration to finalize their divorce. Mediation can short-circuit that schedule at a much lower price.

Probably the major benefit of mediation is lowering the level of hostility inherent in a divorce. Even when mediation fails to resolve all the differences between parties, just the act of dealing with each other in a controlled environment and reaching agreement on some issues can reduce the amount of animosity in the process, along with the expense.

Warren Cole, a mediator with Piro & Lilly in Houston, often feels the need to remind the parties what they have to win or lose from this process.

"When people fight over property," he says, "one party usually feels he or she is giving too much and the other party is not giving enough. To break through the barrier, I tell them you can give a little more to settle it or pay $20,000 to $30,000 to litigate this case. In the long run, you'll be better off with mediation."

Beware of Mediation Abuse

Critics of the mediation process often ask pointed questions that highlight weaknesses in this system. For instance, how do you reach a fair settlement when one side hides assets or vastly underestimates his or her financial position?

A party who hides something or otherwise negotiates in bad faith can abuse the mediation process. The theory behind mediation is a sound one. But like many good things that come into use on a large scale, those who manipulate the system can abuse the mediation process.

Having your attorney on hand should protect you from those abuses. In many cases, discovery is completed prior to mediation and you have the opportunity to determine the value and character of all assets. In some cases, mediation can cost as much as you would spend by going to court.

Sometimes, mediations break down because of disagreements over values. This often happens when a closely held business is involved. For example, a man who ran a paper company and wanted to continue running it after the divorce valued the business at $2 million. His soon-to-be ex-wife valued the same company at $17 million. He wanted to give her other assets worth $1 million for her half of the company's value. She wanted half the value she gave the company, or $8.5 million. Each party brought a business valuation expert to court to justify the numbers. With no one willing to budge, there was nowhere to go but the courthouse.

Sometimes a party will mediate without enough information and accept a bad settlement just to get it over. Women's rights groups have questioned the value of mediation for this reason.

Claiming that women are more often passive partners, they believe that women succumb to the pressure of making an agreement because that's what you are expected to do in mediation.

Even with all the potential problems associated with mediation, we've seen clients go into the process skeptical of the other side's motives and still come out with a worthwhile settlement.

The Role of Your Attorney in Resolving Disputes

Your attorney's primary role in a contested divorce is to provide you with fair but aggressive advocacy that will permit you and your spouse to reach a negotiated settlement. If the other side makes unreasonable demands, however, the attorney must be prepared to go to trial.

In mediation or other types of alternative dispute resolution, your attorney should give you a realistic evaluation of the case. By realistic, we mean that pouring money into extensive litigation is not likely to give you a substantially lopsided property division. Those costs will rise if you insist on making unreasonable settlement demands and reject reasonable ones.

But if you are so distraught or exasperated that you are willing to accept almost any settlement offer just to get a quick divorce, your attorney should be the voice of reason, keeping you focused on the long-term effects of the outcome.

Your attorney should consider the following questions when advising you whether to settle or try your case:

- Will facts harmful to you be revealed at trial?
- Will the parties make credible witnesses?
- Will the other witnesses be credible?

- Will expert testimony be necessary and at what cost?
- Who is the opposing attorney and how much ability does he or she have?
- Will the law or the facts of your case be difficult to explain to a jury?
- What county will the case be tried in and will its local rules or juror pool put the client at a disadvantage?
- What judge will try the case?
- Are there any problems with the admissibility of important evidence?
- Can your separate property assets be traced adequately?

Your attorney should be able to use the answers to these questions to determine a fair resolution of the case, since he or she approaches the problem without your emotional involvement.

CHAPTER 8

HANDLING TEMPORARY MATTERS

WHETHER OR NOT YOU ARE THE ONE who wants the divorce can affect how things go for you in that difficult time between the filing of the divorce and the signing of the final decree by the judge.

If the divorce is your idea or it is by mutual consent, chances are that you will be prepared for the dysfunction of this in-between time. But if the divorce is a surprise to you, and you aren't prepared for it, count on a period of chaos in your life.

Spouses who don't normally pay the bills or keep close tabs on the money often find themselves without the resources for a comfortable life at this difficult juncture. Hopefully, this won't be you.

In a functioning relationship, couples look out for each other, making certain bills are paid, groceries are purchased and incidentals accounted for. But divorce and being functional don't always go together, and some spouses completely disregard the welfare of people they've lived with for decades. They have moved on and you haven't. In this instance, you will want your attorney to request help on your behalf. Your attorney can often handle this by simply calling the opposing attorney and negotiating temporary relief.

If your attorney is not able to forge an agreement on temporary matters with the attorney for the other side, Texas courts have the power to grant you temporary relief and order your spouse to comply.

Three types of relief are the temporary restraining order, temporary order and protective order. Which type of relief the court issues depends on what you request and the circumstances of the case.

Temporary Restraining Orders

The most common procedural device employed in a family law case is the temporary restraining order (TRO). By definition, this order restrains or prevents another party from doing certain things to the person or property of the party asking the court for the order.

The TRO can restrain a spouse from any offensive, profane or threatening contact with the other spouse or children, from physically harming them or from making offensive or repetitious telephone calls.

The TRO can also restrain a spouse from destroying, selling, concealing or encumbering any property, including one party's separate property, falsifying documents or needlessly spending money.

You can also restrain the other party from moving your children outside the state or county, removing them from school or day care or hiding them.

Temporary Orders

While the TRO says what you can't do, the temporary order tells what you must do. Among the items covered by these temporary orders are requirements to:

- Inventory all property
- Pay temporary child support
- Pay interim attorney fees
- Pay temporary spousal support
- Appoint parents as conservators of the children
- Award use of property, including homes, automobiles
- Operate a family business
- Divide debts
- Provide visitation with children
- Produce documents

Protective Orders

An ex parte protective order is issued in an emergency and is designed to protect the applicant or a family member from domestic violence. This order may force the other spouse from the home without a hearing if the complaining spouse signs an affidavit providing a detailed description of the circumstances and testifies at a temporary ex parte hearing.

For the court to order a person excluded from his or her home without a hearing, the complaining spouse must have lived at the residence within the past 30 days, there must be clear evidence that the person to be excluded has committed family violence during the same time period and there must be a clear and present danger that the person to be excluded is likely to commit further violence.

Since a temporary ex parte protective order is only valid for 20 days, a hearing during that time will determine if a final protective order is issued. At the hearing on an application for a protective order, the court must find whether family violence has occurred or is likely to occur in the future.

The protective order is a serious maneuver that sparks a quick police response in the event that it is not obeyed. Violation of a protective order is a Class A misdemeanor, unless the defendant has previously been convicted two or more times or has violated the protective order by stalking or assaulting the other party. In this event, the offense is a third-degree felony.

Generally a protective order will last two years. In such an order, the court may require the person found to have committed violence to complete a battering intervention and prevention program, attend counseling and perform other acts. Further, a protective order may prohibit that person from communicating with anyone protected by the order, going near the residence or place of employment or business of a protected person and harassing or following him or her.

Contested Temporary Hearings

Even though a judge may issue a temporary restraining order, a hearing will be scheduled within 14 days to determine whether to continue the order. Most often, both sides will agree that any injunction in the case will be mutual. Temporary hearings can be expensive and time consuming, but they are often needed to force one of the parties to do something necessary or refrain from doing something else. At a temporary hearing, one side in the divorce may be ordered to pay living expenses for the other spouse, pay child support or maintain and pay for health insurance, among other things. A temporary hearing may also address such matters as custody and possession of the children, interim attorneys fees and who will live in the marital residence before the divorce is final.

HE SAID
SHE SAID: To Her a Drunk, To Him a Loving Dad

He said he came home one evening to find that she had taken the kids and left. When he tried to contact them, she wouldn't answer her cell phone.

She had done this before. She would eventually come home, he thought. Sometimes she overreacted when he came home after a night out with the boys, but she would come home when she ran out of money, if for no other reason. He was tired of explaining where he'd been and what he'd been doing. She was always lecturing him about his responsibilities to the family. But he paid the bills and made it home when he was needed. She couldn't understand that sometimes after a long day at work, he just needed to blow off steam.

For the last few months, she bugged him about his drinking. He didn't have a problem. When you're a problem drinker, you're drunk at work or take a drink when you first get up in the morning. He wasn't like that. She was just growing more uptight the longer they were married, and it was ticking him off.

Sure, a few times he drank more than he should have, especially when they were out with friends. She said he embarrassed her. He hated going to dinner with those people anyway.

Their arguments had escalated in the last few months. He was depressed after being passed over for a promotion at work. Drinking a few beers when he came home at night allowed him to forget how much he hated his job. She said he was drinking too much and taking his frustrations out on her and the children.

To keep her from griping at him, he quit drinking at home. He spent his evenings with buddies at their favorite bar. But, surprise, she complained about that. He hated coming home because they would argue. He found it more difficult to control his temper when she started on him.

Days passed after she left and didn't call. He started searching for her, but none of her friends would tell him where she was. Then he received divorce papers that included a temporary restraining order and an order keeping him away from her and the children until a hearing was held. Had she lost her mind? He'd never been violent with her or the kids.

She said she lived for years denying his drinking problem. When she was a child, her father came home every night and enjoyed a couple of beers before falling asleep in front of the TV. She was accustomed to grown men passing out in their favorite chair. But her father was a mellow drunk; he was not.

When they went out with friends, he drank too much, got loud and annoyed everyone. Their friends quit calling and inviting them out. She was tired of explaining his behavior.

The last few months, he drank even more. He masked his frustration over his job, but she could not get him to open up and talk about his feelings. His behavior was destroying the family. The children were frightened of him.

When they heard his car pull into the driveway, they disappeared into their bedrooms.

She was sympathetic to his problems. She understood that he hated his job and was disappointed about the promotion he didn't get. When she suggested they attend family therapy to work out some issues, he refused. How do you help someone who won't allow himself to be helped?

She could feel him pull away. She feared that one of these evenings, he would lose his temper and hurt someone. To protect herself and her children, she asked him to stop drinking in their presence. The suggestion enraged him. He shoved her against the wall, screamed in her face and raised his fist. She couldn't remember the last time she'd been that frightened.

How do you have the patience or willpower to continue dealing with this? The thought of leaving him scared her. She didn't know if she could raise the children by herself. But she was tired of living in fear.

Following another contentious evening, she took the children and left. She feared how he would react, so she devised a plan. They would settle in with her sister and she would contact a lawyer.

She confided in the family law attorney she hired that she feared her husband would violently oppose the divorce. Could they do anything to keep him away from her and the children while the divorce was pending?

The result was that he drove away everyone he loved. She considered him a threat to her safety, and the more she thought about it the more frightened she became. He decided everyone was overreacting. At a hearing on the family violence protective order and temporary support, he would show them how reasonable he could be. He didn't look like the monster she described to her attorney, in his suit and tie, and she feared no one would believe her.

She told the judge about her fears and about the one night he almost struck her. After all the evidence was presented, he was ordered to pay temporary child and spousal support and attorney's fees. She received temporary primary custody of the children and the house during the divorce. He was awarded standard visitation with his kids. A permanent protective order was not granted, but the message came through to him. This was a serious and disheartening end to his marriage.

CHAPTER 9

FINANCES IN THE SHORT TERM

THE FINANCIAL ASPECTS OF DIVORCE come in waves at the beginning of the process. First come the filings from one side. Then the other side in the dispute files an answer to the original petition for divorce. Shortly thereafter, each party begins to request information from the other party. Both parties may become sufficiently incensed because they ask for information that one side or the other may not want to give but that may be important to the case.

With all this paper flying, the situation feels like retaliation that is often financial. One spouse retaliates by refusing to pay some bills, giving access to accounts or charge cards or selling off certain assets. If taken to its extreme, this financial punishment can strap one of the parties so completely that the other side can apply pressure and force the cash-poor party to accept an unfair settlement.

The spouse with less income needs to develop a safety net of protection from a financial catastrophe. Safety net resources can come from savings accounts, use of credit cards, assistance from family members or friends or even short-term loans.

Use of Joint Accounts

While it is perfectly legal for you to take money from a joint account or obtain a cash advance from a joint credit card if you are a signatory on the account, be ready for the other side to question your motives. If you utilize any joint funds, account for how you use the money. Judges understand when you use this money for groceries, rent or other essentials. You can tarnish your reputation if you plead poverty, then take a trip to Las Vegas or buy yourself jewelry with money that also belongs to your spouse.

Joint Credit Card Debt

Most people think that if a joint credit card becomes a problem during the divorce, they can simply close the account and that will stop the headache. Unfortunately, the account is not actually closed until the balance is paid. Even after that happens, credit card companies are happy to reopen accounts. If you cannot pay off and close the account immediately, here are some possible solutions:

- Agree with your spouse to use joint funds to pay off the debt, then close the account.
- Apply for a separate credit card for each of you. Split the balance between the two accounts.

- If your spouse can't qualify for credit alone,
  perhaps a relative or friend can co-sign on a new card,
  then he or she can transfer part of the balance.

Paying Bills During the Case

It's always preferable for the two parties to agree on which debts will be paid by whom. But if you find it impossible to reach agreement, the court may order that one party or both pay the bills.

At several points in this book, we emphasize that if your spouse fails to pay the bills allotted to him or her, and your name is also on the note or credit account, the lender can still come after you to pay the debt. The court has no authority to order the mortgage company or other lender to release one of its borrowers. Many divorcing people labor under the misconception that when a judge says you are off the hook, there's nothing the creditor can do. But your contract with the creditor predates the court proceeding, and people cannot avoid their contractual obligations simply by getting divorced.

CHAPTER 10

DISCOVERY

YOU MIGHT ASSUME that if a man and a woman know each other for two decades, they would learn everything about each other. But when a divorce takes place between two people, there is always new information to gather.

That's why we engage in discovery, which takes place in most civil lawsuits, including divorces. During discovery, parties to a lawsuit gather and disclose information — financial and otherwise — before a trial can take place. Theoretically at least, discovery is meant to avoid trial by ambush.

In some family law cases, both spouses are asked not only to produce documents and records, but also to respond to questions both orally and in writing. It is an essential part of jurisprudence that both sides provide full information and documentation to serve as a basis for meaningful settlement discussions or for going to trial.

Depending on the relationship of the lawyers and the two parties, discovery may be as informal as a telephone call or letter, or as formal as receiving reams of paper detailing requests from the other side. Only by approaching discovery and disclosure in the spirit of cooperation can parties reduce the time required and the cost of the case.

Understanding and keeping up with the discovery process is very important in divorce cases. The best way to do that is to have strategy sessions with your attorney about what information is being sought and why.

Hiding Money, Finding Assets

How could your spouse stoop to hiding assets that would normally be part of the divorce settlement? If your marriage reaches meltdown, that's exactly what could happen. And the tell-tale signs are classic. If you know that your spouse makes a good living, but an inventory of his or her assets shows almost nothing of value, income or assets may be stowed away from view for use after the divorce is final.

In most cases, finding hidden assets is not difficult, if the assets exist. People usually don't get very creative with their hiding places. It's often less about offshore bank accounts than money hidden in plain sight.

A prime example is the doctor whose wife knew he was not declaring all of his assets, but she just couldn't prove it. Once they owned a sizable collection of modern art paintings and sculptures, but during the marriage he told her that he sold most of them to cover shortfalls in the payroll at his medical practice. That seemed like a plausible explanation at the time, but under the microscope of divorce his every move merited examination.

The woman's attorney asked if her husband carried a brief-case, and she said he had one by his side at all times. He kept it in a safe at his office and locked it in the trunk of his Mercedes-Benz roadster when he went out.

Since the Benz was registered in both their names, the woman could legally enter the car and check out the contents of the briefcase. She had a duplicate key made, followed him to the golf course and took the briefcase out of his trunk. Inside, she found bankbooks showing millions of dollars on account. She also found a key ring. The keys, it turned out, opened a private storage locker where his beloved art was stashed.

While the woman was certainly never in danger of being destitute, even if the assets remained hidden, finding the assets made a big difference in her lifestyle. Now the pressure was not as intense, and she could move forward into her future. Hidden assets do not always have a profound effect in a case, but they can be helpful most of the time.

You and your attorney should make every effort to uncover hidden assets. There is nothing less satisfying than signing an agreement knowing the person you made a deal with is cheating you of community assets. While it is better to discover the chicanery while you are negotiating the divorce, all is not lost if you uncover the property after the fact.

Hidden assets are undivided assets. You can petition the court to divide them later, if you find them, as long as there aren't any "catch-all" provisions in your divorce decree. For example, if your decree awards your spouse all bank accounts in his or her name, discovering an account later that you didn't know existed wouldn't help you very much. If, however, your spouse signed, under oath, an inventory saying that a list of accounts was complete, you may be able to lay claim to the newly found assets. A person who denies the existence of property that belongs to others may be guilty of fraud. If you find these assets during the time period allowed to appeal your divorce, merely discovering them can be the basis of the appeal. You can also place a penalty clause into your divorce decree stating that any undisclosed assets must be awarded to the other spouse.

Here are some other ways that people hide assets:

- Pay off a phony debt to a friend or relative.
- Pay expenses for a girlfriend or boyfriend, such as college tuition, gifts, travel and rent.
- Delay bonuses, stock options, raises or other employment benefits until after the divorce.
- Set up a custodial account in the name of a child who will be your dependent.
- Skim cash from a business he or she owns.
- Pay salary to a nonexistent employee.
- Pay money from the business to a friend or family member for services never rendered, expecting the money to be given back after the divorce.
- For a business owner, delay signing long-term contracts until after the divorce.
- Fail to report antiques, artwork, hobby equipment, gun collections and tools.

Make an Inventory

To keep track of assets, investigate your personal and business finances before filing for divorce. As discussed before, make copies of important documents such as tax returns for the past several years, bank account statements, pay stubs and other documents that reflect joint assets or debts. Keep these documents in a safe deposit box or at a friend's house if you are living with your spouse. Don't forget to check the tax returns for any loss carryforwards. These can be of great value and should be part of the settlement negotiations.

Try to inventory your community assets before the divorce gets heated. List the most valuable assets and take photos of them if you can. Remember, knowledge is power.

Your attorney will give you an inventory and appraisement form to detail just about everything you own. This is the first step in the discovery process. In Texas, both spouses are generally required to complete and sign this form under oath and exchange it with the other side.

Formal Discovery

In addition to exchanging inventory and appraisement forms, the financial information necessary to go to trial or settle a case is transferred from one party to another through several discovery tools used in Texas family law. Those tools include the following:

Interrogatories — These are written questions from one party to the other. Answers to them are given under oath and usually must be prepared and sent to the other party 30 days after the request. Interrogatories may include questions relating to a party's employment and salary information, bank accounts, charge accounts, assets and debts. You may be asked what persons have knowledge of the financial facts of your case. Since interrogatories are issued early in the process, sometimes you can catch the other side unaware of the consequences of an answer. Of course, you may also have to answer interrogatories. If questions are directed at you, discuss the inquiries with your attorney to determine the best way to respond.

Request for Production of Documents — This contains specific demands for certain documents needed for the preparation of a case. Usually, you ask for two to five years of bank statements, tax returns, charge statements, business records, insurance information and financial data, documents supporting separate property claims and any evidence the other party plans to use at trial. In most cases, if you fail to produce a document when requested, you will be prevented from using it in court. A responsible attorney will object at trial to the admission of documents he or she has been unable to examine because the other side didn't produce them.

Request for Admissions — These are written questions in which you ask a party to admit or deny pertinent facts in the case. For instance, your attorney may ask the opposing party to stipulate that a piece of property is actually your separate property and not part of the community estate, since it was acquired prior to the marriage or during the marriage by gift or inheritance. This is often used to avoid attorney and expert witness fees when a piece of property is clearly not part of the community estate. If you fail to answer requests for admission in a timely manner, your silence may be considered an admission by the court. This means you cannot simply avoid answering questions without negative consequences.

Depositions — This is the most confrontational, and often most important, discovery tool, since it is taken in person, under oath, often with the opposing party present. In most divorce cases, a deposition is necessary to discover the basis of the opposing party's case or the substance of the testimony of a witness in the case. Usually, the other side will take your deposition in your attorney's office with a court reporter taking down your testimony. Your lawyer should be present to protect your rights, but the opposing attorney actually runs your deposition, and he or she will ask questions about your finances and the history of the marriage. Your deposition may or may not break your case at trial, depending on how you testify and the particular facts of your case.

You must be prepared to name every reason you want the divorce if you plan to utilize these reasons at trial. As with interrogatories, you are often asked to name every person who has knowledge of your case and what he or she will testify to at trial. Working with your attorney, you should prepare for your deposition so you do not forget critical parts of the case under the pressure and intensity of the moment.

There are numerous strategies for handling a deposition, and your attorney should advise you of the impact of your deposition and the questions asked.

A deposition can be a shortcut to discovering the opposition's entire case. In a large property case several years ago, the wife filed a vicious and accusatory pleading alleging wrongdoing by our client. Her attorneys simply filed the pleading as a tactic, hoping to put the husband on the defensive. Instead, we took her deposition at the start of the case and learned that the wife had no facts to support her claims.

The wife and her attorneys were put on the defensive and stayed there throughout the case. A deposition can be used to discredit a witness who changes his or her testimony at trial.

Good lawyers use the deposition process to size up the opposing party and determine how the person will appear on the witness stand. It is important to prepare for your deposition and make notes of what was said in it for use at trial.

Often a party will use the deposition to scare the opposition, giving a taste of the confrontational atmosphere you can expect in an actual trial. This lesson can be expensive but effective for the person scheduling the deposition. Depositions usually require the services of a court reporter, who makes a transcript of the testimony, and a lawyer, who must spend time preparing for it. Before you decide to take the deposition, make certain a settlement can't be reached beforehand and that the information you might get is worthwhile. One deposition can cost you several thousand dollars to complete.

If you want to find out about a bank account with a few hundred dollars in it, there are other ways to get the information. If you suspect the existence of an account with thousands of dollars hidden away in it, or if custody of your children is at issue, a deposition can be a good investment. For more on preparing for and executing a deposition, check Appendix D at the back of this book.

Electronic Evidence

For some family law clients, the most prideful moments occur when they play a successful game of "gotcha," getting the goods on the other side in a divorce or child custody case through telecommunications, computers and other high-tech means. Unfortunately, those moments are also fraught with anxiety for those attorneys familiar with the Federal Wiretapping and Stored Communications Act and state laws in this same area. In family law cases, clients may be motivated to record telephone conversations of their spouses with third parties or access email or voicemail communications. In this modern age, spouses are increasingly searching for proof of the other spouse's infidelity or gaining favorable evidence by reading emails, wiretapping the home telephone, eavesdropping on cellular phones, or retrieving records from internet conversations in chat rooms.

The legality of these actions and the usefulness of evidence gathered this way are complicated matters. If the retrieved messages are stored on a home computer that allows equal access by both spouses, there may be no violation of law. Federal and state wiretap statutes regulate the recording of telephone and face-to-face conversations and accessing email and voicemail. Both federal and Texas statutes prohibit the electronic interception of a voice communication unless at least one party to the communication knowingly consents to it. One notable exception is when one parent tapes a conversation between the other parent and a minor child. Even though neither party to the conversation knows about the taping, state courts assert that the parent doing the taping has authority to vicariously consent for the minor when it is perceived to be in the best interest of the child.

A divorce lawyer should know the law applicable to electronic eavesdropping. Improper retrieval of electronic communications may constitute a violation of law that carries criminal and civil penalties. More important to your divorce case, though, your attorney must understand the admissibility of the evidence and how a judge or jury will perceive it. Will it come across as conclusive proof of your contentions, gathered legally, or will it be petty snooping that invades the privacy of the other party?

Talk to your attorney about the complete range of effects before gathering electronic evidence.

Much easier to gather and often more valuable are communications through the new range of social media -- MySpace, Facebook and Twitter, just to name a few.

Although each of these media became popular through their use by teenagers and young adults, the extraordinary growth in Facebook the last few years has been with middle-aged people and older. Members "friend" each other by the thousands, and sometimes those are old girlfriends or boyfriends or people they were otherwise attracted in high school, college or early in their work careers.

Facebook may seem harmless, but we know a case in which a man posted a photo of himself with a woman obviously vacationing in an exotic locale and that turned out to be the first real evidence of an affair.

Likewise, a man intercepted one of his wife's truncated Twitter messages:

"It's off to lunch with Ben and then we'll take the rest of the afternoon."

"Who's Ben?" the man wondered.

CHAPTER 11

FINANCIAL PLANNING

ONE OF THE MOST PRODUCTIVE STEPS divorcing people can take during the process is to consult a financial planner. A professional financial advisor can provide useful information that reduces the tax consequences resulting from settlement decisions, helps minimize budget expenses, develops income options and plans major financial decisions such as retirement or home purchases.

Friends, relatives or your attorney may provide you with the names of reputable financial planners in your area. Working together after the divorce, you and your advisor may decide to retain certain assets or sell others.

14 Suggestions for Your Financial Security

Because many of our clients are high-net-worth individuals, we often suggest they work with financial planners to ease the transition from married to single life. We compiled the following 14 valuable suggestions for reaching financial stability from several of these planners:

1. Before filing for divorce, try to increase your emergency funds as much as possible. This should be above and beyond the money you need for regular expenditures. Excess liquidity can only help. After the divorce, some people with extra money go a little crazy, taking exotic vacations and buying fancy cars. Don't deny yourself unreasonably, but set proper limits.

2. Be prepared to pay for the best financial, legal and accounting advice. Don't be turned off because a professional has a high hourly rate, if the advice you get is worthwhile. Faulty advice costs more in the long run.

3. People in the midst of divorce sometimes get preoccupied and forget to pay bills on time, and that can hurt your credit. It's one thing if you cannot afford to pay your bills on time. It's another if you forget to pay them. Repair your credit if it has been damaged and check your credit often if you think your ex may have done something to harm it.

4. Seek out financial planning advice before negotiating a final settlement. You probably need expert help to determine how the settlement will affect your future plans. Projections should focus on income and expenses, retirement and insurance needs.

5. In your settlement, push for liquid assets or those with low tax liabilities. Settlements that appear 50-50 may not be equal due to tax consequences.

6. As you settle the divorce, factor in long-term care needs. If you are fairly young and in good health, long-term care insurance is relatively inexpensive. If you are 50 years old or older, look into a policy.

7. If you have special-needs children who will be disabled in their adult lives—requiring your continued care—address their lifetime care in the settlement. If they are not eligible for Medicaid, potential expenses should be taken into consideration in the settlement agreement. Life insurance can help you cover this future liability as well.

8. Try to determine either the amount or percent of college costs each parent will pay. If your children are quite young, you might be able to contribute to a 529 college savings plan.

9. If you receive spousal support or child support over time, make sure the payor is covered by adequate life insurance. As time passes and the amount of the obligation lessens, the insurance amount can be decreased if you structure this through multiple-term policies. For instance, you could purchase $1 million in coverage the first 10 years, then reduce it.

10. If one party has stock options that may not be worth much today, either have an independent evaluation done to determine how to factor them into your settlement or divide the net proceeds from them in a certain manner.

11. Change your will and beneficiary designations as soon as possible after the divorce. Most people fail to remember that. Also, address beneficiary changes for retirement plans and variable annuities.

12. Both parties usually lose financial footing in a divorce, and both former spouses must work to make up the loss. It takes discipline to get back on track to your retirement and financial security goals.

13. Learn to make your own money decisions with the help of a financial planner. If your former spouse made these decisions for you in the past, you will have to take on this task.

14. Don't make any sudden major changes for at least one year following the divorce. Taking risks may seem exciting, but divorce is risky enough. It takes time to adjust to the financial realities of life after divorce.

CHAPTER 12

Other Professionals Your Attorney May Enlist

DIVORCES THAT INVOLVE intricate negotiation sessions can benefit from the services of professional consultants and decision makers. Other than financial planners, the professionals who contribute to your financial well-being are lawyers in other legal practice areas, accountants, estate planners, appraisers, business valuators and even family therapists.

Other Legal Specialists

Your attorney may need to hire specialists in other areas of the law to help you with matters outside family practice. For instance, if there is substance abuse or other criminal behavior in the family, you may need help from a criminal lawyer. If you need to know the tax consequences of an action or how to divide a business, you may want to employ a business or tax attorney. You may need a corporate transactional lawyer who can determine the validity of documents or draft them for you.

In Texas, most family law specialists work in small firms that handle just family law cases and not a full range of legal services. Under these circumstances, your attorney may have to go outside his or her firm to hire professionals from those other legal disciplines.

Because family law contains elements of many areas of the law, specialists in this area have a wide range of legal knowledge. Few attorneys are able to be experts in tax or criminal law as well as a top family lawyer. There is a difference between bringing in a specialist who can take care of a single difficult matter and following a team approach.

Only the largest, most complicated cases require an entire team. In those cases, your attorney should operate at the head of the team, taking advice from one or more other attorneys.

For instance, Michelle Mendez is a top Dallas attorney we often call into a case if our client or the other party is contemplating bankruptcy. As a specialist in this area, she can evaluate if bankruptcy is the right move for our client or how such a filing by the other side could affect our case.

"Divorce sometimes forces people into bankruptcy," says Mendez. "If the person you were married to or recently divorced from files for bankruptcy protection, this can have a direct impact on your financial well-being."

Accountants

Accountants can estimate the tax consequences of many different options available to you while negotiating your divorce settlement and determining when and how tax returns should be filed and how to properly prepare them.

"A settlement that appears to be a fair division of property from a financial point of view may turn out to be not so equitable when tax issues are calculated," says Hunter Nibert, a certified public accountant in Dallas. "Say a divorcing couple has $200,000 in assets — $100,000 in a 401(k) and $100,000 in a brokerage account that is not tax deferred, meaning that taxes have already been paid on that money. If one spouse gets one account and the other gets the other one, the brokerage account is worth more after taxes. Both parties received $100,000 on the books, but if you take the money in the 401(k), there are taxes to pay. One hundred thousand dollars on an after-tax basis can yield as little as $60,000. That's the sort of thing people might not consider in the heat of battle."

Accountants might also be asked to take a budget apart and determine the personal expenditures related to it. For instance, he or she can take your home or family financial records and create a spreadsheet that shows your family's average spending per category over the past several years. When one party claims to make less income than the budget allows and has done that over time, then something is amiss. Often that means the person claiming the lower amount is not telling the truth about expenses or has another source of income he or she doesn't want to report. An accountant can determine this from a detailed analysis of income and expenses.

Accountants are also employed to evaluate and audit business financial records to determine if a company is providing benefits and other perks beyond reported income. Examine the actual bank and other financial records to make these determinations. Many times, this type of audit shows that a spouse is receiving reimbursements, bonuses or commissions that are not being reported as income. Adding these payments to a spouse's income can make a huge difference in the amount of assets available for division and can lead to alterations in the amount of child support.

"The CPA is in his element verifying financial statements," says Nibert. "Where you run into difficulty is with self-employed people and small businesses that may be informal with their record keeping."

In the case of a closely held business, Nibert says the amount of compensation paid to an employee-owner often must be adjusted to determine a value for the business. If the employee-owner is a sole proprietor or 100% owner of the company, he or she may take all the money beyond expenses produced by the company as compensation rather than declaring a profit. If someone else owned the company and paid an employee a fair salary, the profit would go to the owner. To determine the value of the business, a valuation expert must arrive at a fair salary, subtract it from the money available to determine the profit earned by the business and factor that into the value of the business. A closely held business can produce large amounts of income and substantial benefits, but may have no excess funds because of this control over compensation.

Family-owned and other closely held businesses often pay personal expenses for owners and employees who work in the business. If those personal expense amounts are paid out of the business, be prepared to substantiate that they are not personal income and should not figure into child support and other calculations. Many spouses working for these types of businesses use business accounts to pay for vacation homes, personal automobiles and luxury travel. You may need the services of an accomplished accountant to see behind those payments to determine if they are legitimate.

Estate Planners

The estate planning objectives of most divorcing people change once a divorce is filed. Typically, a married couple has a will that states if one spouse dies, all assets go to the surviving spouse.

The transfer of assets between spouses in a divorce is usually done without creating tax liabilities. But the division of certain assets such as family business interests and retirement benefits, family limited partnerships, the structuring of post-divorce payments and the utilization of insurance and trusts present traps for the unwary. And experts who make their living with such transactions must be the ones who run those traps.

An estate planner can take advantage of opportunities to minimize estate and income taxes and control the management and ultimate disposition of assets, including those that must be allocated to divorce obligations.

"People should restructure their wills immediately after they are divorced," says Alan Klein, an estate planning attorney with Klein and Pollack in Dallas. "The plan that was put into place before the divorce might not reflect what the individual wants afterward."

One of the most common estate planning problems Klein sees after a divorce is the failure to make changes in a beneficiary. Beneficiary designations for employer-sponsored plans including group-term life insurance, 401(k) plans, profit sharing plans or pension plans should be reviewed to assure that the correct person or people are designated. The paperwork to make these changes usually must be completed on company forms and submitted to the employer.

"After people go through a divorce," Klein explains, "they are not only faced with the emotional aspects of the divorce itself, but frankly they are tired. They are physically and monetarily spent. They say to themselves, 'I don't have to do something immediately, I'll do it tomorrow.' And then tomorrow becomes a bunch of tomorrows."

Appraisers

When the divorcing parties are unable to agree on the value of a marital asset, an appraiser is often brought in to determine that value. Divorcing parties hire appraisers before they divide assets or when they sell the assets and divide the proceeds.

Real estate appraiser Jim Goodrich says that when one side wants to keep the family home, "That person will tell us everything bad about the home (to keep the value low) and the other will tell us everything good about it (to inflate the value). We are pretty good about sifting through all of that. I'm sure we've had the wool pulled over our eyes before. But we try to filter out what really matters and what doesn't matter."

This method is especially true with the marital residence, but it can also be used with other real estate holdings, vehicles, jewelry and other illiquid assets.

Business Valuation Experts

Divorcing couples with a privately held business interest often hire valuation experts to determine a company's worth.

"Private companies are different from publicly traded ones whose stock is valued on an exchange and the price published in the newspaper," says David Fuller of Value, Inc., of Dallas. "We do an extensive evaluation of the company's financial history and outlook for the future. To accomplish this, we look past the numbers to the structure of the company, the products and services it offers, even its marketing materials, and we use all that information to determine what drives their business."

It's the same information that an investor would use to arrive at a purchase price for a business, the owners of the business would use to formulate a selling price or accountants would use to report the value of a business interest for tax reasons.

The degree of control the divorcing person can exercise over the business affects its value. For instance, if the expert values your business at $1 million and you own 75% of the business, your portion may be worth $750,000. If you own only a 10% interest, you have no control over the pricing of products and services or whether the business makes any major capital expenditures or issues a dividend on stock. In this case, your interest might be valued at less than 10% of the total value of the company.

Another facet of many valuations is determining what constitutes personal goodwill as opposed to company goodwill. In Texas, the courts have generally held that the personal goodwill of a married business owner is not divisible, while company goodwill usually is part of the community property estate. A successful medical practice often presents a good illustration of both types of goodwill. The business valuation expert must determine how much of the practice's success is due to the doctor's rapport with his patients and his reputation in his field and how much can be attributed to the practice's trade name, advertising, good location or helpful staff.

If a case involving business valuation goes all the way to trial, a business valuation expert like David Fuller will follow the steps below to help a divorcing person and his or her attorney determine a company's value:

- Gather documents and other information.
- Analyze the situation.
- Apply generally accepted valuation methodologies.
- Consider valuation issues unique to divorce law.
- Issue a report with a value and its rationale.
- Assist in mediation.
- Be available for depositions.
- Testify in court as an expert witness.
- Work with the attorney to devise a creative settlement.

"The truth is that few businesses are easily divisible," says Fuller. "They are usually the largest asset in a divorce, so if you give one person the business there may not be enough liquid assets to offset the value of the business. Few companies have half their value in cash available." In these cases, the person who receives the business must mortgage some assets not easily convertible into cash or offer money concessions to the other side to make a settlement work.

For business valuators, Fuller says, the most frustrating cases are those where two experts arrive at wildly divergent values. Sometimes inexperienced valuators try too hard to please those who are paying them, but in other cases the experts may utilize completely different fundamental assumptions.

"Say it's a small company that has developed a promising new drug," Fuller conjectures. "One side may look at the situation and say they don't have FDA approval, they can't raise more money and success looks a long way off. Then the other side says this may be true, but think how rich the company will be if the drug ever gets to the market. To get a deal done, one side, the other or both have to come back to more reasonable values. You don't want an expert to pick fights by taking unreasonable valuation positions. If this happens, you may wind up paying exorbitant professional fees and end up with the same value you would have had if you hadn't fought about it."

Mental Health Professionals

While the emotional side of divorce is what counselors and therapists most often address, it's important to note that financial strain causes many dire emotional problems related to the divorce process. You will want to explain what's happening, right from the beginning, to everyone involved.

"I advise couples to tell their children they are not going to have the money they used to have," says Dr. Maryanne Watson. "Children are actually very good team players, if they know what is going on. It's when they don't know that it's a lot more confusing for them. The reality is that they are going to have less. If they can help formulate the solutions, you can elicit their cooperation. Children do best when they have information. They need to be told everyone will have to work together to live on what they have. As long as they have food, clothes and shelter, they can do well. But, of course, this only works when the financial reasons aren't blamed on the other parent."

Clinical psychologist Dr. Ray Levy believes that if the parents are okay, the kids will be fine. "If the parents handle the financial strains okay, then kids will. Kids see their parents adjust and they adjust. They don't really care if parents can't afford things. What they want most is personal attention from their parents. If they have to choose between a new video game or spending time with Dad, they are going to choose Dad. They may not understand when they can't go to camp for the whole summer, but if they knew it meant not seeing their parents, they would want the attention and to stay connected with Mom and Dad."

CHAPTER 13

COUPLES LIVING TOGETHER

ONE OF THE MOST significant financial commitments in America these days involves people who live together outside marriage. This includes couples who are sexual partners but are not married to each other and share a household. They are self-identified as unmarried partners and not roommates.

According to the U.S. Census Bureau, the total number of unmarried couples in 2003 was about 4.6 million, up from less than half a million in 1960. The National Marriage Project at Rutgers University indicates that about a quarter of unmarried women age 25 to 39 currently live with a partner and almost half lived at some time with an unmarried partner. More than half of all first marriages are now preceded by cohabitation, compared to virtually none earlier in the 20th century.

According to the 2000 Census, there were 262,912 unmarried partner households in Texas that included a man and a woman. There were another 47,489 same-sex households in the state.

Just 30 years ago, unmarried couples (either heterosexual or homosexual) living together in a sexual relationship were breaking the law in most jurisdictions. But today many young people believe that living together is natural.

Whether it's productive or not is subject to debate. What's not in question is the fact that breaking up without the legal standing given married people can be a messy affair.

On its most simple terms, what happens if one party, who is paying one-half or more of the household expenses, decides to leave and the other party is unable to pay the bills? What if the financial connections get more complex, such as when people buy homes or automobiles together or establish a joint bank account?

Common Law or Just Unmarried?

How the courts handle these cases depends on whether the unmarried relationship is a common law marriage or two people just living together.

Common law marriage traces back to the early days of the Texas Republic, when most people lived in rural areas. Preachers and judges often covered wide areas and were not always available to marry people. Common law marriage was employed to get the deed done immediately. Today, Texas is one of only 12 states that still recognize common law marriages.

To make a common law marriage valid, the couple must prove the following elements:

• The man and woman (same-sex couples may
  not marry) agree to be married.

- Since making the agreement, they live together in Texas as husband and wife.
- They represent to others in Texas that they are married.

All three elements must exist at the same time for a common law marriage to be valid. These marriages are equivalent to ceremonial marriages in legal rights and duties, and the legal status of parties to a common law marriage is the same as that of married persons.

Common law marriages are not favored in Texas law. The Texas Supreme Court has stated that Texas' recognition of common law marriage is "grudging," although the state has not moved to abolish them.

Disputes between people married under common law are subject to the Texas Family Code and are heard in domestic relations courts and other courts that hear matrimonial law matters. Disagreements between couples who are not common law spouses are treated the same as contractual arrangements. Any civil court in the state can hear these disputes.

Children of the Unwed

Estimates by the National Marriage Project indicate that nearly half of all children today spend some time in a cohabiting family before age 16. Living arrangements get more complicated when unmarried people have children. While an agreement under contract law can settle where your new sofa will reside after a breakup, family law judges look to the best interest of the children when determining where children will live.

For the children of these relationships, the risk of a broken home is drastically increased. Three-quarters of children born to cohabitating parents see their parents split up before they reach 16 years of age, while only about one-third of children born to married parents experience a breakup.

On average, these children display significantly more behavior problems and have lower academic and work performance records than children in intact families. The level of difference depends on the amount of conflict between the parents. Children of unwed parents are more likely to be the subject of child custody battles, conflicts over visitation and child support enforcement fights.

Cohabiting couples should be aware of the high risk facing their children and make therapy and other help measures available to them.

Proving Paternity Now Easier

Several reputable studies show that over the years, children of unmarried unions receive far less child support than those from conventional marriages. Proving paternity is often essential to establishing rights of inheritance and rights to Social Security benefits. About 350,000 DNA paternity tests are performed each year.

Often, fathers simply refuse to believe that these are their children. In other cases, men use the DNA tests to establish paternity and assert their parental rights when the mothers fail to allow them visitation with children they believe are theirs. While most questions of paternity involve unmarried couples, in a few cases a parent in the midst of divorce might ask for paternity testing to establish whether a child of the marriage is the husband's child.

Courts widely accept genetic test results to establish paternity. Genetic, or DNA testing, is quick, inexpensive, and accurate. A small blood sample or a simple swab inside the cheek can be used to prove paternity with 99.9% accuracy. In fact, testing has become so simplistic that test kits are available over the Internet and samples from the child may be taken without the other parent's knowledge.

Proving paternity can have enormous financial implications for the two adults and the child. A lifetime of child support for one child can total several hundred thousand dollars for a middle-class family. In some cases, as a parent you must do DNA testing on a child before four years of age or risk being on the hook for child support when you learn through other means that the child is not yours. When a parent dies, Social Security survivor benefits and private insurance can mean the difference between subsistence living and a comfortable life for a child born out of wedlock.

12 Steps to a More Productive Divorce

1. Establish goals for the divorce. Write them down and remind yourself throughout the divorce. Always refer to these goals when considering any action.

2. Help your attorney organize and collect financial information. This includes establishing online access to financial data so you can check balances quickly for any withdrawals. Run a credit report on yourself. This report lists all accounts, account numbers and balances of those accounts that are open in your name.

3. Complete an inventory of your property. Save valuable time by clearly defining each asset and its value. Also, provide the most recent statement for every account listed in the inventory.

4. Choose your battles wisely. Do a cost/benefit analysis, deciding which assets are important, what they are worth and which ones you don't need. Never spend more money fighting for an asset than it is worth.

5. Divide your assets yourself. Try to work with your spouse and decide who gets which assets.

6. Be realistic about your ability to retain assets. Make certain you can pay for the marital home before accepting it. If both spouses work and still struggle to pay bills, chances are you can't handle them by yourself.

7. Look for resolution, not revenge. Remaining level-headed will allow you to negotiate a settlement faster. Take mediation seriously. It can save thousands.

8. Consider tax consequences. What looks good on paper can end up costing you in the long run.

9. Pay attention to details. Stay on top of your divorce decree and make sure your spouse is following through on his or her obligations. Do not allow too much time to pass before contacting your attorney regarding an enforcement action.

10. If your spouse concedes a point, reciprocate the favor. Working with your attorney and the other side can settle your case faster than heading into court to resolve the issue.

11. Negotiate for the future. When considering a settlement agreement, think in terms of the divorce and potential future litigation. Current litigation can cost a fraction of what you will spend to go back to court and modify an agreement.

12. Get over it. As difficult as this may sound, try to be the mature one in the divorce, working on goals for yourself and your children rather than seeking revenge. Instead of dwelling on the past, move forward with your life.

Part Two
Dividing Assets and Debts

HE SAID
SHE SAID: It's Her Separate Property

<u>She said</u> the land was in her family for generations. As a child, she spent most weekends working the farm and helping her grandparents maintain the farmhouse. To her, the property was more than just a piece of dirt and a house. It was her heritage. Before they got married, her grandparents died and she inherited the place.

For years, they spent weekends at the farm. He suggested they make the farmhouse their home. She loved the idea. A slower pace would be perfect for them all.

But the farmhouse needed significant repairs. He told her he could do them on his own. It was a big job and he wasn't the type of person to maintain focus on the project.

When she told her parents of their plans, they offered to pay for the restoration. Consider it a gift, they said. She thought they were so generous. He thought they were meddling again in their lives, like they did every day since they married. But she couldn't tell her parents no. They would be crushed. She prevailed and the restoration began.

In the early stages of the construction, they fought constantly about her parents' involvement in the project. Since they were paying for repairs, her parents wanted to be included in every decision. The restoration was taking twice as long as anticipated. With each passing month, the tension grew. And their problem wasn't just the farm. They couldn't agree on anything. She knew she'd been spoiled as a child, but he was a handful. She sought advice from her minister and friends. Could these disagreements really harm their marriage?

She approached him about attending couples therapy. He came to a few sessions, but as soon as the topic turned to the farmhouse, he walked out of the session. She struggled to see why he couldn't let go of his anger. Shortly after the failed therapy sessions, he moved out.

She contacted a lawyer and filed for divorce. Her lawyer asked her to list their community property and her separate property. On her separate property list, she included the farmhouse and surrounding property. It was an inheritance and it would remain in her family.

He said that since the day they got married, he worked to maintain the farm and the farmhouse. He put in countless hours repairing what broke or fell into disrepair. He knew she overlooked the little things they did as a couple to maintain the place, but he remembered.

After spending almost every weekend traveling back and forth to the property, he suggested they move out there permanently. They enjoyed the laid-back country life. The only stumbling block was the rundown farmhouse.

He planned on doing most of the repairs himself. There were only a few things he couldn't do, but he could oversee the project. And he would get a great deal of satisfaction from a project like this. That was before she told her parents.

It was a generous gift, but her parents acted so indecisive and cautious. They made the process much more difficult than it had to be. Her parents would not allow him to complete any of the repairs on his own. He knew they were spending way too much money on the contractors they hired, but nobody listened to him.

They argued each day over the progress of repairs. Everyone blamed him, but he felt any progress was due to his attention to matters. He showed his frustration with the way she would stick up for her parents. He no longer saw this as a gift, but a hindrance.

He tried to avoid conversation about the farm. He hated confrontations. Especially when nothing ever got solved. If she could not see his point of view, he just wouldn't talk about it.

He was surprised when she suggested going to a marriage counselor. Sure, they weren't communicating well, but only about the farmhouse. Everything else was fine.

He agreed to the sessions. He was hoping the therapist could referee a civilized discussion on the farm issue. But even with the therapist's help, she still refused to consider that her parents were meddling in their lives. How could she be so blind?

After these worthless therapy sessions, he wasn't surprised when she filed for divorce. His attorney asked him to draw up an assets inventory list and indicate the property that was separate and what was community. For him, the farmhouse was community. Throughout their marriage, he had spent plenty of his time and effort maintaining the place. He was ready to fight for what was rightfully his.

The result was a detailed investigation that involved the use of a forensic accountant. Her attorney told her that Texas automatically assumed everything in the marriage was community property. The burden of proof was on her to show the farm was her inheritance acquired before the marriage. In this case, the proof was easy to obtain since the deed was dated prior to the marriage. His attorney told him that she might have to reimburse the community estate for his time and labor used to improve the property.

He felt confident about his case, but that confidence was misplaced. The court had to consider characterization of the property, the money used for repairs and the increase in value brought about by those repairs. As it turned out, his in-laws paid for the repairs as a gift to their daughter because they feared just this situation. They kept very good records to prove that any major repairs were done by professionals and paid by them. He claimed a certain amount of sweat equity in the place. But because of his inexperience with construction, her attorney characterized it more as weekends playing farmer than actual work. Any increase in property value was a result of the repairs paid for by the parents.

At trial, the farm and the newly renovated farmhouse were deemed to be her separate property and his claim that she reimburse the community estate for his work failed.

CHAPTER 14

DIVIDING ASSETS AT DIVORCE

THE CONCEPT OF COMMUNITY PROPERTY in Texas originated from Spanish civil law, which considered the family a community in itself and an asset of the larger community. The idea was that members of the family should share property generated by the family.

Today, Texas is one of nine states (including Arizona, California, Idaho, Louisiana, Nevada, New Mexico, Washington and Wisconsin) that recognize the principle of community property as it pertains to divorcing couples.

Community property is defined in the Texas Family Code as property acquired by either spouse during the marriage that is not the separate property of one of the parties. Case law has defined community property as any property or rights acquired by one of the spouses after marriage by toil, talent or other productive faculty, and as property acquired during marriage other than by gift, device or descent that is the product of the unique, joint endeavor undertaken by the spouses.

Identify Your Assets

The first step in a successful division of the marital estate at divorce is to identify the assets. In some cases, this is the easiest step in the process. In those cases where the assets are kept secret from you, this step can be difficult. You may have a house, two cars, some rental properties, a 401(k), household items, furniture and jewelry. At this point, you should not worry if a certain asset is community or separate property, what its value is or whether you want to retain that asset in the divorce. Just concern yourself with making sure you know what assets you have and where they are located.

In almost every case, each spouse prepares a sworn inventory and appraisement. This form lists all property and debts, gives each party's opinion of values and states any claims, including claims of separate property.

Phil Fielder of ATECH Information Services locates assets in those cases where a spouse is not forthcoming with basic information. "We find property, vehicles that may not have a lien against them and assets that might not come up in disclosures of community assets. We have situations where a spouse is involved in a lawsuit and they are going to receive a judgment somewhere down the road and we can attach that judgment before it is passed down and the money disappears."

Looking at bank account records, county tax rolls, credit card statements and data retrieved from home computers can produce clues about the whereabouts of hidden property.

"Of course, tax returns are a wealth of information," Fielder says. "They tell what financial accounts people have and if they have other property or another source of income. One woman thought her husband made $50,000 a year and all of a sudden you look and see that he made more than twice that amount."

A wide variety of assets comprises community property that may need to be divided. Any debts or other liabilities associated with these individual assets must also be addressed. The property to consider includes the following:

- Artwork
- Antiques
- Automobiles
- Bank and brokerage accounts
- Boats and trailers
- Business interests
- China, silver, crystal
- Collectibles
- Guns and sporting goods
- Home furnishings
- Life insurance and annuities
- Retirement plans (401(k) plans, pension plans and IRAs)
- Stock options, deferred income and bonuses
- Stocks and bonds
- Tools and yard equipment

Community Property or Separate Property?

An essential part of asset division is determining whether an asset is community property or the separate property of one of the parties. The court can only divide community property. All property that either spouse possesses upon dissolution of the marriage is presumed to be community property unless proven otherwise. Separate property remains with the spouse who can prove ownership.

A spouse's separate property consists of:

- Property acquired by a spouse before marriage
- Property acquired by a spouse during the marriage as a gift or inheritance
- Recovery for personal injuries sustained by a spouse during marriage, except for any recovery for loss of earning capacity during marriage.
- Property that can be traced to a separate property asset.

All income acquired during marriage, whether from separate or community property, is community property unless the spouses have agreed otherwise in a prenuptial or postnuptial agreement. These agreements are discussed in Chapter 28. For example, if the wife comes into the marriage with $50,000 in a brokerage account, any interest or dividends earned on the wife's separate property funds are community property.

Say the wife owns a home that is fully paid for prior to marriage. Once the couple marries, they decide to remodel the home, adding a bedroom and bath and an apartment over the garage. They pay for these additions with a home improvement loan that is repaid from earnings by both parties. Since the couple made no agreements to characterize the property otherwise, the original home is still the separate property of the wife. The community estate, however, may be entitled to reimbursement for the use of community funds to increase the value of the wife's separate estate. After some time, but still during the marriage, the couple decides to purchase another home and make payments on a mortgage loan from renting out their first home. The new home and the income they receive from the rental are community property.

"People don't seem to have an appreciation for the magnitude or implications of the community property presumption," says forensic accountant Doug Fejer. "That's the biggest mistake people make. They think if they have money before they are married, naturally they get credit for it when they divorce. They are always surprised how difficult it is to prove that the funds should remain separate."

When the couple in our example divorces, the wife must show by clear and convincing evidence that the original home is her separate property. In this case, the best evidence may be a deed for the property showing only the wife's name and the date she received title to the property.

Separate property commingled with community property remains separate property as long as its identity can be traced. Where separate property becomes so commingled with community property as to defy segregation and identification, the entire property is community property. Thus, as long as the separate funds can be traced, they may be deposited in an account that also holds community property without losing their character as separate property.

Forensic accountants can be hired to trace separate property.

What Is Your Property Worth?

Before the parties' property can be divided, its value must be determined. In most cases, the parties must provide convincing evidence of the value of their property and be prepared to support those valuations in court. To save time and expense, the parties should agree on the value of as many assets as possible.

It is difficult to attach values with mathematical accuracy. A competent appraisal is based on facts, common sense and informed judgment. The fact-finder, either a judge or jury, determines the value after hearing all the evidence.

The trial court may consider various types of evidence to determine the value of the parties' community property. An owner is qualified to testify about the value of real property if he or she knows the property's market value. Even if the owner fails to qualify as an expert, he or she can still give opinion testimony.

Often the two parties will hire expert witnesses to value their property. The judge may hear this testimony and decide to accept one of the valuations, discounting the testimony of one expert in favor of the other. In some cases, though, the judge will set a value that's somewhere between the two values.

We've even seen a judge accept a property owner's testimony in preference to expert testimony. In one case that involved the value of racehorses, the trial court accepted the testimony of our client, the wife, instead of an expert with advanced degrees in horse management and nutrition. The wife attended numerous horse sales, shows and races. She bought and sold horses, read horse association journals and collected race magazines. We were able to show that she possessed more up-to-date, real-world understanding of the horse business as opposed to the more academic knowledge of the husband's expert.

You will be asked to submit a sworn inventory and appraisement of your property as evidence in your trial. If the opposing

party does not contradict your inventory, it may constitute suffi-
cient evidence for the court's valuation of the parties' property.

You may enter into evidence such documents as mortgage
instruments, sales and earnest money contracts, receipts and
bills of sale. Market quotations, tabulations, lists, directories or
other published compilations generally relied upon by persons
in particular occupations are also admissible. They may help
to establish the values of such property as stocks, crops, motor
vehicles, antiques, gems and precious metals, livestock and pedi-
greed pets.

Although the court determines the division of community
property, a jury can value the property and that is binding on the
court in a divorce proceeding.

The Property Division

With your community estate identified, characterized and
valued, you might think the property division is easy. You would
be wrong in many cases. The property division can be the most
difficult part of reaching settlement.

Pride, ego and the need for revenge often cause perfectly
mature people to become unreasonably petty, fighting over
property they didn't even use during the marriage. If you don't
want the judge telling you whether you get to watch the flat
screen television or play with the Xbox, convince your soon-to-
be ex that the two of you should divide the assets yourselves.

If the worst human traits govern your attempt to divide
household goods, we often recommend a formalized selection
process of alternate selection. If you hit an impasse, begin this
process by making a list of only the remaining disputed property.

Flip a coin to determine who selects first; the winner chooses one item of property from the list. The other party then picks an item from the list and the process is continued in turn until all items are selected. Under this procedure, you can select property in any way you like — the most expensive items on the list, the items you want or those you know your spouse wants. You can select items one by one or a room at a time. The selection process remains balanced because of alternate selection.

Letting the Court Decide

No matter how formalized your process of dividing property, some couples simply can't make those decisions together. That's when judges step in and undertake the division. When making this division, the court may not divest a party of his or her separate property. The court has the authority to set aside a separate property homestead for a set period of time or for the benefit of the children while they are minors. For example, if a couple's marital residence is the separate property of the man, the judge can create a separate property homestead so that the woman can keep their children in the home until they reach 18 years of age.

"We became involved in what I call 'pots and pans' cases," says former judge Susan Rankin. "One case I heard is typical so far as scheduling is concerned. We spent three-and-one-half days deciding child custody and visitation, which was very important. That left us Friday afternoon to divide the property, and it gets chaotic if you try to do it right in a couple of hours."

Rankin emphasizes that you must inform the judge if you want a particular item of property. Judges will do all they can to accommodate the wishes of the parties, if they know those wishes.

When a court divides community property, it should determine if the property can be partitioned "in kind," the preferred method of dividing the estate. If a marital estate consists of four automobiles that are fairly equal in value, one very valuable home, one less valuable home and some home furnishings, the judge might divide this estate as follows: One spouse would receive two automobiles and the most valuable home. The other spouse would get the other two automobiles, the less valuable home and the home furnishings. That might happen if the judge is inclined to divide the assets equally. If the property cannot be divided in kind, the court may appoint a receiver to sell the property and divide the proceeds.

Dividing Assets in a "Just and Right" Manner

Under Texas law, the court may consider several factors when awarding one spouse more than the other spouse. Those factors include:

- Education of the parties
- The parties' respective earning power
- The parties' business and employment opportunities
- Disparity in the parties' incomes or earning ability
- The parties' physical health
- The parties' ages
- The parties' different needs for future support
- The award of custody of the parties' children
- The relative sizes of the parties' separate estates

- The parties' relative financial condition and obligations
- Length of the marriage
- Fault in the breakup of the marriage
- Either spouse's dissipation of the estate, including excessive community property gifts to others or waste of community assets
- Benefits the party not at fault would have received from continuation of the marriage
- Nature of property to be divided
- Tax consequences
- Attorney's fees
- Fraud on the part of one spouse

The court may award a money judgment in favor of one spouse as a means of dividing the marital property. This solution may help a spouse recoup the value of that share of the community estate lost though the other spouse's actions. Also, if one spouse is awarded a particularly valuable asset, such as the family home or a business interest, the court may make an equalizing award of cash to the other.

"… a room is not a house
And a house is not a home
When the two of us are far apart
And one of us has a broken heart."

Luther Vandross
"A House Is Not A Home"

CHAPTER 15

DEALING WITH THE FAMILY HOME AT DIVORCE

THE FAMILY HOME is more than a house. It's also more than a simple asset. In most cases, it is the emotional and psychological center of family life and is much prized by both spouses in a divorce. That's why so many divorcing couples fight over the home only to find that neither of them can afford to keep it after the divorce.

How the home is handled and who ultimately winds up with the residence often depends on who can afford to pay for it after the marital assets are divided, debts are paid and child support is ordered.

Even though you may want the home and feel you deserve it, you'll want your attorney and financial advisor to examine your financial ability to maintain the residence before recommending how you should deal with it. Realizing you cannot afford the home may be tough for you, but it is better to learn this fact early. You don't want to spend time formulating a strategy that involves fighting for an asset you cannot keep.

From the day you or your spouse files for divorce, the home becomes an issue. The amount of financial resources available in the marriage often determines how the home is treated at the outset. In most cases, the party with temporary custody of the children maintains temporary possession of the home because it is the children's residence.

No matter what you do with your home on a temporary basis, you eventually have to decide how to deal with this most prized asset. Your choices follow.

Your home may be your most valuable asset

Say you sell the home and come out with $150,000 after paying off the mortgage and deducting the costs of sale. It would stand to reason that each party would take $75,000 from this transaction. But say you also have two automobiles, some household furnishings and a 401(k) with a total value of $50,000 after paying off loans that secure some of these items. The marital estate is worth $200,000, but because of several factors the court decides to give one party 60% of the assets, or $120,000, and the other side gets 40%, or $80,000. To accommodate that split, one spouse may receive $100,000 in cash from the sale of the home, one fully paid off automobile worth $15,000 and some household furnishings. The spouse who gets 40% of the assets receives the remaining $50,000 from the home sale, an automobile worth $5,000, the remaining furnishings worth $10,000 and the 401(k) worth $15,000.

Sell the Home and Divide the Equity

A common way to divide this asset is to place the home on the market, sell it and divide the proceeds between the parties. In most cases, this is part of the overall settlement, so you decide whether one party gets all the proceeds of sale or you can divide it in some pro-rata fashion.

Getting two divorcing people to settle on a selling price for the home can be a difficult task. Under ideal conditions, you are trying to sell the home for the fair market value. This value is defined as the amount a willing buyer would pay to a willing seller who desires to sell but is under no obligation to do so.

To determine the fair market value, the court may hear evidence of the following:

Market data — Evidence of recent comparable sales in the area is evidence of market value.

Tax value — Because property is to be appraised for tax purposes at fair market value, the taxable value of property may provide evidence of the fair market value of property.

You can probably verify that value by consulting a realtor. You may not incur the cost of an appraisal because most realtors know local market values. This is helpful when there are few properties comparable to your home now on the market.

"If it's not an amicable divorce, the people may not communicate with each other about the home," says Jan Richey, an agent with Keller Williams Realty in Plano. "So we have to talk to one and then talk to the other, then talk to their attorneys. It makes our job more difficult, especially when they have to sign papers. One won't sign unless the other side does something for them. So we encourage them to call us when they reach an agreement."

Occasionally, each of the parties may decide to conduct an independent appraisal of the property. If the two appraisals are significantly different, the parties can select a third appraiser to value the home.

A realtor can help you decide what repairs and improvements should be done to the home before the sale. If that realtor is selling the home, he or she can usually arrange for work to be done on the residence at a reasonable price.

The settlement agreement should specify who pays the mortgage, taxes, insurance and utilities before the residence is sold. The agreement should tell who provides routine maintenance and upkeep, as well as who pays the cost of heating, cooling, roofing and structural repairs.

The agreement should also require the person who lives in the home to keep it clean and orderly, ready to be shown, while it is on the market. Once again, the realtor can outline the sales strategy that will make the home most appealing to potential buyers.

"Often, the spouse who stays in the house is the one who didn't want the divorce," says Richey. "The other party is paying the mortgage and the one in the house doesn't want the house to sell because they are living there free. They won't make the home accessible, nor do they keep it clean or take care of the home. They want to make the other person pay, and this is the best way to do it."

Determine Net Equity in Your Home

An agreement should specify that when the home is sold, all costs associated with the home or other debts in the marital estate be deducted from the gross sales price. Those costs may include:

- Mortgage payoff
- Brokerage commission and costs of sale
- Reimbursement to one of the parties for repairs or improvements on the home to facilitate the sale
- Unpaid property taxes
- Payment of other debts specified in the settlement agreement

The settlement agreement should state whether to hold the equity in escrow or divide it between the parties in some manner.

Appoint a Receiver to Sell Your Home

To avoid any foot dragging on the sale of your home, you might want to include a receivership provision in your decree. If the home is not sold within a specified time frame, or the parties cannot agree on a sales price or the manner in which they will sell the home, the court may appoint a receiver to sell the home. Proceeds of the sale are used to pay off the mortgage and closing costs and the remainder is divided between the parties. Typically, a local real estate agent is selected to serve as receiver and his or her commission constitutes the fee.

This should be a last-ditch effort, because a court-ordered sale rarely brings the maximum price. If there is little equity in the home and a significant amount of mortgage debt, this may be the only option available to get out from under that mortgage.

If one party inhibits the sale, the threat of a receiver selling the property may provide the necessary incentive to prevent this behavior.

Transfer Interest in Your Home from One Spouse to the Other

In some cases, one party wants so badly to retain the family home that he or she gives up more assets than necessary just to keep it. As part of the overall settlement agreement, one party may transfer his or her interest in the home to the one determined to keep it. The party who gives up the home usually gets a larger share of cash, retirement accounts, household items or a family business. Giving up ownership of the home may be a smart move, because the home may not be worth as much as the other spouse thinks it is or market conditions may make a quick sale difficult. Both parties should know what they are getting or giving away under this arrangement.

The agreement should also specify that the parties execute the necessary warranty or quit-claim deeds to transfer interest and clarify responsibility for mortgage debt as well as taxes and other expenses. The parties in a divorce need to understand that even if you transfer the asset to your ex-spouse in the settlement agreement, you are not absolved of responsibility for the debt unless your spouse refinances the loan or sells the property and pays off the loan.

In Texas, the spouse who is awarded the property routinely signs a deed of trust to secure assumption in favor of the other spouse. This means that if the owner spouse fails to make loan payments, the non-owner spouse can force a foreclosure and pay off the debt. This protects the non-owner spouse from having a judgment or delinquency placed on his or her credit report because of the action (or non-action) of a former spouse.

If the debt is not repaid, the mortgage obligation remains on both parties' credit reports and has to be addressed in future loan applications. This can sometimes be handled by showing the creditor a copy of the divorce decree indicating that the other spouse is responsible for the debt.

Depending on the amount owed and other circumstances, you might want to compare the value of staying in the home while leaving the mortgage in place versus selling the residence to clear up that obligation. If you compare household expenses to a monthly apartment rental, you may find your mortgage payment is less than the going rate for a similar-size apartment in your area. These comparisons are a large part of the analysis you must make early on to determine whether to keep the home. You may believe that you can't afford the family home, but other housing options in the area may be even more expensive.

Temporary Use by One Spouse

Divorces never happen at an opportune time, especially in the lives of children. One settlement option is to have the parent the children will live with most of the time occupy the home for a set period of time after the divorce. The home is then sold and the equity divided in the manner specified in the agreement.

For example, you may have one child who is a junior in high school and another who will enter high school in two years. Requiring these children to pack up and move to a new residence can disrupt their lives. To minimize the disruption, you and your spouse might decide that you stay in the home with the children until the older child graduates. You can move during the summer, when the younger child is transitioning to a new school anyway and the older child is getting ready for college or another inevitable life change.

Your settlement agreement should specify how long you have use of the residence and what events trigger sale of the home. The agreement should spell out who is responsible for the mortgage payment during this period and who provides routine maintenance and upkeep, as well as necessary repairs.

How the equity is divided at the point of sale can be an issue. If one spouse pays the mortgage payments and other costs over a two-year period or more, then the situation gets more complex. Most homes appreciate in value over time. In many cases like this, the party paying the mortgage and other expenses wants to get credit for the increased value. To calculate the appreciation, one option is to set a value at the time the agreement is made and subtract it from the amount received from the home at sale time.

This situation can be handled smoothly if it is specifically and accurately set forth in the agreement.

When a Judge Must Decide

For a variety of reasons, divorcing couples are often unable to agree. That's when you go to trial on these matters, and the judge gets to decide how you deal with the family home.

In Texas, a family court judge has the authority to impose any of the remedies listed in this chapter. If the home is a community asset, the judge may order the home sold and the equity

divided or awarded to one party. Sometimes, the home is awarded to one party and that party is responsible for the mortgage
payment. Or the judge may determine that keeping one party in
the home for a certain number of years is best, with the residence
being sold at the end of that time and the equity divided.

Consider Your Housing Options

You really do want to evaluate your housing alternatives
before deciding what to do with your home in the divorce. We've
seen people give up their home only to find that an acceptable
replacement was not available at a price they could afford where
they wanted to live. This is especially critical for families with
children. After you identify an acceptable price point, answer the
following questions:

- What type of housing fits your lifestyle (home,
  townhouse, apartment)?
- Are those housing types available where you want to live?
- How much does housing cost?
- Is the housing in your current school district
  or another comparable one?
- Do you have enough cash for the down payment,
  closing costs, possible improvements and the first
  mortgage payment?
- What type of mortgage is available?

"Divorcing families almost always move down in house
size," says Jan Richey, "and all you can do is find them a smaller
home. How much smaller depends on the price of homes in

their neighborhood. A lot of people we help live in posh areas. Sometimes they can't maintain their lifestyle or stay in the same school district. With a divorce, it takes longer than normal for reality to set in than with an amicable family relocation."

Even though she sells homes for a living, Richey sometimes counsels divorcing clients to take stock of their situation before buying a home on their own. "Typically, the person who did not want the divorce is still grieving and should not be making one of the most expensive investments in life immediately after the divorce. They should probably rent or lease and work through the grieving process before going out and trying to make a financial decision like that."

Plano mortgage broker Mike Wolfe says people who buy immediately after the divorce need to be realistic and not set their sights on the most expensive home in town. At one time, you could do what is called a 'no-doc' loan, where the mortgage company didn't verify assets, income or employment for people with 5-10% of the purchase price for a down payment. That was before the housing bubble burst. Today, unless you are putting a huge amount of money down, almost all loans require a good credit rating and a credit score well into the 700s.

Tax Matters Related to a Home

The tax consequences associated with the transfer or sale of the home to a third party could affect the value of the award. There is no gain or loss when the transfer of property takes place between spouses or former spouses. However, your capital gains tax exposure should be considered. In Texas now, homeowners can use the equity in their homes to pay off other bills. This is often better than cashing in a retirement plan that might have a penalty for early withdrawal or a more heavily taxed account that includes stocks and bonds. In some cases, you can even deduct the interest you pay on a home equity loan from your taxes. You need to consult a tax expert and consider all possible moves.

Play It Safe: Do a Title Search

Before you sign a settlement agreement that includes disposition of your home, review the loan documents and do a title search to make certain no liens have been placed on the property without your knowledge. We've heard several variations of the following story: a young mother receives the home when she and her husband divorce. She makes just enough money to pay the mortgage and upkeep on the home for the first year. But then, one day she receives a notice from her mortgage company that her loan carries an adjustable rate and the payment is going to almost double the next month.

She is upset with her husband for choosing the adjustable rate loan without explaining the downside to her, but she simply decides to sell the home, take the equity and find something affordable for herself and her children. She lists the home with a realtor and sells it in two weeks, with closing set for 30 days later. She is happy to get her asking price so she has some money to relocate, and she decides to bank the proceeds and rent an apartment until she finds the right home.

A week before the closing, her realtor calls to say that a required title search uncovered two liens on the property from judgments recorded against her ex-husband. She has no way to satisfy the judgments, which are for more than her equity. At closing, she has to sign over all the proceeds from the sale of her home to the creditors. She is left with no money and no way to purchase a replacement home for her family.

If you are deeded a home, don't just assume that you are receiving a valuable asset. The young woman in our story can avoid this problem by doing a title search before accepting the home in the division of property.

HE SAID
SHE SAID: Who Can Afford the Family Home?

<u>She said</u> that she always dreamed of having a home with a big backyard. When they got married, she saved every spare dime for a down payment on their first home.

And they purchased a fixer-upper for a good price. She was thrilled. He wasn't so sure, and he talked about the money pit this house could become. She figured once they moved in he would relax and enjoy their new home. They could easily afford the mortgage payments with both of them working. But when the twins came two years after their daughter, she quit her job to care for their children and they began to live on one paycheck.

Raising three young children and juggling a tight household budget wore on their relationship. They fought often about money or repairs on the house. She was the only one who did anything to improve their home environment. He would plan a project, then not follow through; it was always up to her to finish.

The tension around the house was unbearable. She couldn't remember the last time a simple discussion did not turn into an argument. She said they needed a separation so they could work on their problems. To be truthful, she was tired of pretending they were a happy family.

Six months after they separated, she filed for divorce. She knew times would be tough. As long as she could keep the children in the family home, though, everything would be all right.

He said she was on his case about buying a house from the moment they said, "I do." He enjoyed the little responsibilities they had with no children, no house and no worries.

But she was determined to own a home, and he wanted to make her happy. The money they saved was enough to buy a rundown old home that needed a lot of work. Once they closed on the house, he knew he would never have a lazy Saturday afternoon again.

He worked long hours to make ends meet. But she was relentless. No matter how many hours he worked during the week, she had repair projects planned for evenings and weekends. He finally had to confront her. He was not taking on another project. She was the one who wanted the house, now it was her job to maintain it.

To be honest, he was relieved when she suggested the separation. He didn't want to be the one blamed for the end of their marriage. When she served him with divorce papers, he figured they had given their marriage a good run. Now it was time to part ways.

The result was a divorce that divided their only asset, the house. They didn't have anything else to split, and there wasn't much equity in the house. She was adamant about keeping the old place. No way was she moving her children to a new neighborhood. They were already dealing with enough following the breakup of the marriage.

He thought they should cut their losses and sell the place. They both needed money for living expenses and to pay attorney's fees. There wasn't any spare money between them, but she was relentless. They finalized their divorce by agreeing that she should keep the house. She didn't count on having to reimburse him for half the equity, but that was a price she was willing to pay at that moment.

Six months after the divorce, after trying to hold things together, she finally sold the family home. She had no other choice. She simply could not afford to keep it on her own.

CHAPTER 16

DIVIDING THE FAMILY BUSINESS

THE MOST PAINFUL PART of the man's divorce was selling his company. This story, from an article in *Inc Magazine* about divorce-proofing your company, gives an idea of just how difficult it can be to divide what is usually the largest asset in a marriage.

He founded his automobile-service business during the mid-1980s. It experienced tremendous growth as his marriage was deteriorating. Even worse for him, he failed to predict both how successful his company would become and how ugly his marital breakup would get.

The man didn't take the most basic precautions to ensure survival of the business in the event of a divorce. Since the couple lived in a community property state, she was entitled to half of everything. Most of their assets were in the business. To come up with the cash necessary to settle the divorce, it became obvious that he had to sell his business. He received two offers on the company. One was for considerably more money, but it involved a long-term payout. She didn't want to take a risk that the buyer might not come through over time, so he was forced to accept the lower bid, which was a cash offer.

Who Gets the Business?

Not all cases involving a closely held business result in sale of the company, especially if the business owner engages in a little premarital divorce planning. When the business is owned prior to the marriage, we find that a prenuptial agreement between the divorcing parties or a partnership agreement among the business owners can eliminate most problems. You can also place your business assets in a family limited partnership to benefit children of a previous marriage.

When one party can prove he or she owns the business prior to marriage, only the earnings from the business during the marriage are community assets. If a family limited partnership is in place prior to the marriage, only the earnings from the divorcing parties' share of the partnership during the marriage can be divided in divorce.

Most businesses created during the marriage are awarded to the party running the business. By this arrangement, the non-owner spouse receives one of the following: other assets to offset the value of the interest given to the business owner, a cash settlement from money borrowed by the owner spouse or payments over time. Very rarely will a judge divide a functioning business between two antagonistic spouses in a way that requires them to cooperate in the running of the company after their divorce, although the parties may inflict such an arrangement upon themselves to keep the business intact. Businesses with multiple owners usually avoid the uncertainty of domestic relations court by instituting shareholder or buy/sell agreements that restrict the transfer of equity ownership.

"These agreements define the procedure for any change of ownership," says Barry Hardin, an attorney with Vincent, Lopez, Serafino & Jenevein in Dallas. "It can be a divorce, death, disability, bankruptcy or a number of other triggering events. Most business owners are resistant to any ownership interest being transferred outside of the initial core group of investors. So they usually have buy/sell agreements in place that give the people in the original group rights of first refusal to purchase the interest if it could be transferred to anyone, like a divorcing spouse, who is not well known to the ownership group."

It's important to maintain stable ownership, especially in the case of start-ups or venture-capital-funded companies.

Valuing the Business

Because the value of closely held businesses can be manipulated so readily, the court often needs definitive evidence from business valuation experts to determine a value.

These are small companies not listed on any stock exchange. You can't merely add up the value of stock like you can with a publicly traded company. The spouse who wants to keep the business usually places the lowest possible value on the business, even if that business provides very well for the family. If the value is low and that spouse has to compensate the other for half the value, he or she has to come up with less cash if the other side or a judge accepts the lower value. There may be perfectly good reasons for the business to be valued low. A new product may fail or most of the business's value may be associated with the owner spouse's personal goodwill. The spouse who doesn't want to operate the business often hires an expert who values the business as high as possible. He or she sees how lavishly the firm provides for the family and wants the appropriate amount of money from it.

Valuations are challenging for both the family law attorney and the expert hired to value a business or professional practice.

An audit of business records is necessary to determine the company's worth. At the very least, your attorney should examine tax returns and other corporate documents, including profit and loss statements and records used to secure financing. In more complex cases, a business appraiser looks at the following information to form an impression of the value:

- The nature and history of the business
- Its tangible assets
- The earning capacity of the business
- Fair market value of all assets
- Amount of goodwill with customers and suppliers

The lawyer must gain some understanding of the possible ranges of value of the business from the expert to analyze a settlement or assess the likely outcome at trial. Somewhere along the way, the parties to the divorce, a judge or a jury must be persuaded that a certain value is reasonable.

HE SAID
SHE SAID: Dental Practice A Major Asset

<u>She said</u> putting him through dental school was one of the most difficult efforts of her life. Between studying and completing the required internships, he didn't earn any real money. She kept them afloat financially. He promised that once he completed his degree, their money worries would be over.

She helped him open their first office shortly after his graduation. To keep employee overhead low, she worked three days a week as office manager. She didn't mind the work. They were building this practice together. She thought it was as much her business as it was his.

After six years in business, the practice flourished and they opened another fully staffed clinic on the other side of town. She took pride in the success of their family business but felt she had earned some time off. It was only right that she enjoy being the wife of a successful dentist.

She put her efforts into redecorating their Highland Park home. Here she hosted lavish cocktail parties, networking with their well-connected friends and neighbors. Even though she was not in the office every day, that didn't mean she wasn't working on their behalf.

It was only natural that he should attend the parties and mingle with their friends. But he complained that he didn't feel comfortable around that crowd. The art of schmoozing with these people was lost on him. He would make an appearance and retreat to his study.

She despised that room where he spent most of his time. She begged him to spend more time with her, but he grew more sullen and withdrawn.

One evening, he came home from work and told her he was closing the second office. She couldn't remember the last time he openly talked about the practice with her. He told her the stress of operating both offices was too much. She offered to return to her old position to help out, but he brushed her off with a wave of his hand.

She could feel the distance growing between them. She spent more time with her friends while he locked himself away in his study. She pleaded with him to attend marriage counseling, but he refused to talk about their marital problems. As time passed, she could feel the cracks in their marriage widening until she could no longer imagine them going on together.

He surprised her by offering to move into an apartment. She was certain he would file for a divorce and she wanted the upper hand. The next morning, she called a divorce attorney her friend recommended. She told the lawyer that she didn't care about the house or the car. She wanted to make sure she got her fair share of their dental practice.

He said his years in dental school were hard for him too, but he didn't complain about that period in their life at every cocktail party. He knew she did a lot for them, but he hated her martyr act.

When he opened the practice, he had no idea what to expect. When she offered to work in the front office, he agreed, although he was concerned about how well they would work together. He was pleasantly surprised to see she ran it so efficiently that he never had to worry about the accounts or insurance claims.

The practice was doing better than he ever imagined. After five years, it generated substantial profits. That's when she began to lobby for a second office. His gut instinct told him to wait a few more years. But she insisted they could double their profits. She got the accountant on her side and kept at it until she finally wore him down.

Just when they opened the new office, she decided it was time for her to retire. He thought she would grow restless after a few months and come back to work. He began to think otherwise when she started interviewing office managers to take over her position.

Because of her retirement, his pocketbook took a hit. It was amazing how much money she could spend in one week. She made things worse by taking shopping trips with her friends to New York and Paris. Their home looked fine, but she began to redecorate it. When she finished, it no longer felt comfortable to him.

He could tolerate her spending and redecorating. But he hated the parties she threw. He never liked her new friends. She would plead with him to attend, constantly harping on him about the importance of networking. He told her she did enough networking for them both.

With the pressure of maintaining two offices, he worked closely with his accountant to improve profits. He wondered how he could provide the lifestyle she had grown to love. It annoyed him that she never asked about the practice. As long as the money flowed, she didn't seem to care. She wanted the money from his business, but she complained constantly that all he did was work. If he didn't work, she couldn't play. Their arguments always led to days of silence around the house.

He finally decided to close the second office. And he made up his mind that he wanted out of the marriage. They had grown apart. He could no longer communicate with her. Every discussion ended in either tears or a screaming match. Most nights it was a little of both.

At his first meeting with his attorney, he explained that he wanted her to have the house, her car and some cash. He wanted sole ownership of his practice. She may have helped start it, but it would be nothing without his name and degree tied to it.

The result was warfare over the family business. Both sides wanted the same thing. And since they had no children, splitting the practice became the focus of the divorce.

He felt that by giving her the house, he should be able to keep her from taking a portion of the practice. How could she think the practice would survive without him? She felt she had put as much of herself into the practice as he had. She didn't understand why he should benefit solely from the profits of business in the future.

He knew the current status of his practice. With the closing of the second office and the lost time connected to the divorce, revenue was down. His expert placed a value on the practice of $500,000. She could only remember when the two-office practice provided a lavish life for them. She valued the practice at $3.5 million.

Each of them brought their attorneys and business valuation experts into court to divide the estate. There the judge set a value for the practice that was closer to his valuation. The rationale was that much of the value was the result of his personal goodwill, as opposed to the goodwill generated by other factors (location, good staff, advertising). In Texas, the personal goodwill of one party is not usually community property. The judge also threw their other assets into the pot, including the house, both their cars and some retirement accounts.

In the end, she retained the house and her car and he was ordered to pay her half of the assets over time.

He kept all rights to the business.

Favored Business Entities

The specific form of the business may affect its value and divisibility in a divorce. The most common forms include:

- Sole Proprietorship
- General Partnership
- Limited Partnership
- C Corporation
- S Corporation
- Limited Liability Company (LLC)

Sole Proprietorships — A sole proprietorship is the simplest business entity and is often operated in an informal manner. There is one owner who may operate financially out of a personal bank account and physically from a desk in an extra bedroom. The sole proprietor receives all the profit from the venture and is personally responsible for all business debts. In addition, this sole owner is personally liable for any damages the business might cause. Because of its simplicity, the sole proprietorship is the easiest form of business to divide in a divorce — if you can trace the business dealings and substantiate the value.

The rules for characterizing business assets in a sole proprietorship are simple. Such businesses created during the marriage from community funds are part of the community estate. If one spouse begins such a business before marriage or with separate funds during marriage, that business probably is the separate property of the business owner. But the profits created by the business and additional assets acquired by the business are community property.

General Partnerships – A general partnership can be a very complex entity formed with two or more individuals, corporations or limited liability companies. Such a partnership is an entity distinct from its partners. Property of the partnership does not belong to the partners, but to the partnership. Even if a married couple comprises a partnership, the court cannot award specific partnership property to either party, as the property is owned by the partnership.

For instance, two spouses may be the sole partners in a general partnership that owns a fleet of transport trucks. When the parties divorce, the partners cannot simply divide the trucks in a way they consider equitable without first dissolving the partnership. They can only divide their interest in the partnership that owns the trucks. If a man is in partnership with several other people and he divorces, the parties may agree to split the partnership interest or the judge may award part of it to the man's wife if this is not prohibited by the partnership agreement. Your attorney can help you divide an interest in a partnership.

Each partner is generally responsible for income taxes on his or her share of the partnership income. If the partnership has losses, each partner may deduct a pro-rata portion of the loss.

Even though there are specific rules for the transfer of partnership interests, the attitude of the other partners can determine how easy it is to make productive use of those interests. If you accept a minority partnership interest in your divorce settlement, the actions of the other partners can affect the value of your interest. The partners may not want to buy out your share or you may get responsibility only for the debts of the business. Look closely at the situation before accepting such an interest as part of the settlement.

Limited Partnerships – This form of partnership is more specialized and structured and includes two categories of partners: a general partner and a limited partner. The general partner has unlimited liability for the debts of the partnership while limited partners usually have no liability beyond the amount of their ownership. The general partner has expansive management responsibilities. A limited partner usually does not have any management responsibilities or involvement in the day-to-day operation of the business. Because a limited partnership interest is more narrowly written than a general partnership interest, being a limited partner may give a spouse tremendous safety and financial security. It could also award a title that carries little or no authority to influence a change or receive any financial benefit.

Your attorney should examine the limited partnership documents and determine what interest is transferable under the partnership and if accepting such an interest is a good decision.

Corporations – A corporation can be a small business with one shareholder or a multinational company with publicly traded stock and thousands of shareholders. The following defines what stock is community property and what is separate property.

Under the inception of title rule, stock in a corporation that was incorporated during marriage is community property.

Stock acquired before marriage, or during the marriage by gift or inheritance, is separate property. Any increase in the value of corporate stock belonging to a separate estate due to natural growth or the fluctuations of the market remains separate property. If the increase is due, at least in part, to the time, toil and talent of either or both spouses, the stock remains separate property, but the community estate may have a right to reimbursement.

Like a partnership, a corporation is a legal entity with an identity separate from its owners. Shareholders of the corporation do not individually own the corporation's assets and generally are not responsible for corporate debts. Following are the two most common types of corporations.

C Corporation — This is the simplest type of corporation. With a C Corporation, the business entity itself owes federal income taxes on earnings. The divorce court has the authority to award a spouse's corporate ownership to the other spouse. If the other shareholders own a majority of the stock and don't want to cooperate with the spouse who received the stock interest, that spouse cannot control ownership of the company. You need to get a clear understanding of the assets and debts of the business, as well as what the corporate documents provide.

S Corporation — This is perhaps the most common form of corporate entity for a closely held business. A sole proprietor may convert his business into an S Corporation for income tax planning and liability purposes. With an S Corporation, the profits and income tax liabilities flow through to each individual stockholder on a pro-rata basis. The corporation itself does not pay federal income taxes.

Examine the corporate documents to see how an ownership interest is handled. If you hold a minority interest and the corporation is not publicly traded, that ownership interest could be of little value. But many S Corporations are very successful and a spouse's interest in the business can be worth quite a lot. Even if your spouse doesn't believe the business interest is worth much, other members of the business community may be willing to pay for it. If the corporate documents allow for the transfer or sale of your interest, you could receive tremendous value for it.

Analyze the actual value of the corporation to determine if this is an interest worth pursuing.

Limited Liability Companies – A limited liability company (LLC) is a relatively new business entity that combines elements of a partnership and a corporation. Like in a corporation, the liability is limited to a member's individual investment in the entity.

This type of entity is common for professional organizations such as medical practices and law firms. The task of dividing the assets of an LLC at divorce is apparent in these professional types of businesses. An attorney or a surgeon may own an interest in a limited liability company, but it would be impractical or prohibited for the attorney's spouse to own or control that interest. It is the particular skill of that professional that makes the LLC valuable.

Unless the spouse has the same skill, the spouse's interest is worth considerably less under his or her ownership. It's usually more worthwhile for a spouse to receive other assets or payments over time for part of the ownership interest, rather than a share of the limited liability company.

The same questions that apply to LLCs are relevant to other business entities. What interest in the enterprise can and would you receive? What is that interest worth? Can you sell it now or must you hold it for a time? If the interest is not easily transferable when you need the money, what other assets are available in the marriage to compensate you?

All of the issues presented here should be examined in close detail with your legal counsel to determine what options are available for ownership of various business interests. Choosing the correct entity from the start will make things much easier.

Tax Liabilities of the Business

No matter what form your business takes, there are always tax ramifications. You may have little knowledge of the business or its tax history and the divorce agreement may say your spouse is responsible for tax consequences. Nonetheless, the Internal Revenue Service may declare both of you responsible for any liability. If so, you may be required to seek relief from the divorce court and the specific language of the agreement will become critical. The agreement should state that the responsible spouse will hold the other harmless for any future problems that relate to income tax liabilities.

CHAPTER 17

EMPLOYEE BENEFITS/RETIREMENT AND BEYOND

MANY EMPLOYERS ARE CHANGING the structure of their compensation packages. In 2006, Verizon, IBM, Sears and Hewlett-Packard froze their pension plans, deciding that their traditional pension plans were simply too expensive to maintain. Other employers have since either frozen or terminated their pension plans, especially since the economy began to go south. Freezing a pension plan is different from termination. A frozen pension plan does not continue to accrue benefits, but the assets remain in place. If an employer terminates a pension plan, the plan must pay out all the benefits as soon as administratively feasible.

In 2006, the Pension Protection Act was signed into law. The Pension Protection Act was meant to help ensure the financial viability of pension plans following high-profile plan terminations and freezes. A few of the Pension Protection Act provisions have resulted in businesses either shying away from adopting new pension plans or terminating/freezing those that were being maintained. With this trend, employees are relying on defined contribution plans such as the 401(k) and 403(b), as well as their own IRA's, and employers are creating and implementing other forms of compensation. These other forms of compensation include incentive bonuses, signing bonuses, retention bonuses, creative stock option plans, and employment incentive agreements/plans.

Characterization and Division of Assets

Most retirement benefits contain community property even if the employee spouse started in the plan prior to the marriage and/or will continue in the plan after marriage. Statutes and case law provide legal guidance for the division of retirement plans, but the issues are often complex.

The buyout of a retirement plan from one spouse to another creates its own set of complex issues. As a result, often the community property portion of a pension retirement plan is divided equally, even though the remainder of the estate may be divided unequally. With regard to defined contribution plans such as 401(k)'s and 403(b)'s, and IRA's, spouses can more easily negotiate a buyout or a court easily make an unequal division, taking into account the necessary tax considerations. It is important to analyze whether a spouse has removed funds or borrowed from a defined contribution plan because a spouse's consent is not required for either. If a spouse has taken a loan from a contribution plan, it is important to consider whether the value of the plan includes or excludes the loan so that the plan is properly valued.

Characterizing other forms of compensation (i.e. incentive bonuses, signing bonuses, retention bonuses, employment incentive agreements/plans) as either community or separate property can be difficult. It is clear that income received before marriage or after the divorce is the earning spouse's separate property. It is problematic when a contractual right accrues to a spouse prior to marriage, or is based on performance prior to the marriage, but the income is received during the marriage. Further, when a contractual right accrues to a spouse during the marriage but the money will not be received until after the divorce, and/or is based on performance after the divorce, characterization problems arise.

Case law is developing in states all across the country on this matter and it is only a matter of time before Texas develops case law with regard to the characterization of these forms of compensation. Interestingly, a look at the case law in other states with regard to these other forms of compensation shows that courts are analyzing the characterization and/or division of these other forms of compensation by using their stock option law or a hybrid of it.

Options Not Just For Wealthy

Stock options present their own complex set of issues and the legal guidance for stock options can be found in the statutes and case law. Employee stock options are no longer reserved for the executive suite.

According to the National Center for Employee Ownership, as many as nine million employees participate in some 4,000 plans. A decade ago, only one million U.S. employees had them. There are two common types of stock option plans: nonqualified stock options and qualified, or "incentive," stock options (ISOs).

ISOs qualify for special tax treatment. For example, gains may be taxed at capital gains rates instead of higher, ordinary income rates. Incentive options go primarily to upper management, and employees usually get the nonqualified variety. Unlike ISOs, nonqualified stock options can be granted at a discount to the stock's market value. They also may be transferable to a spouse, children or charity, provided the employer permits. Dividing stock options that are not transferable requires substantial detail in the final decree of divorce to ensure how the transfer will occur, the taxes to be paid (and at which spouse's rate) and by whom. An employee stock option gives you the right to buy ("exercise") a certain number of shares of your employer's stock at a stated price (the "award," "strike," or "exercise" price) over a certain period of time (the "exercise" period). Tax consequences can be complex. Unlike the case with nonqualified options, an ISO spread at exercise is considered a preference item for purposes of calculating the dreaded alternative minimum tax (AMT), increasing taxable income for AMT purposes. Remember that even if you keep the stock you purchased, you will still have to pay taxes.

There are three main ways to exercise options. You can pay cash, swap employer stock you already own or borrow money from a stockbroker while simultaneously selling enough shares to cover your costs. It is usually smart to hold options as long as you can. Conventional wisdom holds that you should sit on your options until they are about to expire to allow the stock to appreciate and, therefore, maximize your gain, but this wisdom may not breathe success in all cases. In any event, you should not exercise options unless you have something better to do with the realized gain. However, there may be compelling reasons to exercise early. For example, you may have lost faith in your employer's prospects; you are chock-full of company stock and want to diversify for safety; you want to lock in a low-cost basis for nonqualified options; or you want to avoid entering into a higher tax bracket by waiting.

Orders to Divide Retirement/Employee Benefits

Depending on whether the employee spouse works for a state or federal government agency, there are many governmental plans at the state (e.g., Texas Municipal Retirement System, Teacher's Retirement System, Employees Retirement System) and federal (e.g., Federal Employees Retirement System, Civil Service Retirement System, Thrift Savings Plan, Federal Employees Group Life Insurance, railroad retirement, military benefits) level. The plan in which the employee participates will determine the type of order that must be drawn to divide the plan in a divorce. Similarly, when an employee works for a private company where the plans are usually defined benefit type plans (e.g., pension, cash balance pension), defined contribution plans (e.g., 401(k), employee stock purchase plan, employee stock ownership plan), or a hybrid of both types of plans (e.g., money purchase plan, target benefit plan), the type of plan will determine what type of order will be necessary to effectuate the transfer of the benefits to the nonemployee spouse.

Division orders in the private sector are called "Qualified Domestic Relations Orders" and similar orders are used in the other sectors. All retirement division orders are complex and vary significantly from plan to plan. Employers usually have a model order, but using a model order can be dangerous in that the model order is written to make things easy for the plan, not provide the necessary benefits and features for the nonemployee spouse. For example, when dividing defined benefit pension plans it is necessary to address the survivor benefits (pre-retirement and post-retirement survivor annuities), temporary supplemental benefits, cost of living adjustments, and early retirement subsidies, which are often not addressed in model orders.

When dividing the traditional defined benefit plan, the nonemployee spouse can choose to receive the funds under a separate interest order or a shared payment order. Under a separate interest order, the nonemployee spouse may choose to collect the benefits when the employee spouse reaches earliest retirement age (with a reduction for early retirement) and in such case the nonemployee spouse's benefits will be actuarially adjusted for his or her lifetime, and the nonemployee spouse may chose the benefits in any form allowed by the plan. Under a shared payment order, the nonemployee spouse must wait until the employee spouse retires before receiving benefits, must receive the benefits in the same form as the employee, and the benefits are based on the employee's lifetime, therefore there is no actuarial adjustment.

You should expect in your case that an expert will be hired to draft the retirement division order(s) for the nonemployee spouse and another expert to review the order(s) for the employee spouse. These orders often take substantial time to complete since they must be reviewed by and qualify with the administrator of the retirement plan. If such retirement division orders are not completed when the divorce is completed, it may be necessary to file an additional lawsuit for the court to have jurisdiction to sign a retirement division order.

Loans, Taxes and Penalties/Retirement Plans

It is possible to borrow from a defined contribution retirement plan that is qualified under ERISA, such as a 401(k), according to the terms of the plan for loans. IRA's are not ERISA-qualified plans, so you cannot borrow from your IRA and there is no relief for the penalties for early withdrawal. An IRA, however, can be transferred to the other spouse in a divorce without tax consequences for the transfer. A loan against a retirement plan does not trigger the 10% penalty as long as the funds are paid according to the terms of the loan. If the funds are not paid according to the terms of the loan, the unpaid loan proceeds will be treated as a distribution to the employee in the year of default, the 10% penalty will apply, and the employee spouse will receive a 1099-R for the funds in default.

Borrowing from a defined contribution retirement plan is an excellent way to obtain funds for attorney's fees and obtain money for a loan to purchase a home. There are significant tax benefits to borrowing money from yourself for a home, which can be discussed with your certified public accountant. On the other hand, do not use this type of loan to pay off the nonemployee spouse in a divorce because that spouse can obtain the funds via a Qualified Domestic Relations Order and not be subject to the 10% penalty the *first* time the funds come out of the plan, although taxes have to be paid. The one-time forgiveness of the 10% penalty is one of the primary benefits of a Qualified Domestic Relations Order. Funds paid to the nonemployee spouse via the Qualified Domestic Relations Order are subject to the nonemployee spouse's tax rate at the time the funds are paid.

"Fifteen or 20 years ago, when you negotiated a property division, most pensions were pretty much thought of as an absolute guarantee. Now you're looking at them as 'Is this the next Enron?'"

Ike Vanden Eykel
Personal Finance column
The Dallas Morning News
March 14, 2004

HE SAID
SHE SAID: Sometimes Forgotten Assets

He said for the first 15 years of their marriage they worked together as a team. She took care of the house, worked part-time and volunteered at their children's school while he earned a good living for their family.

He worked hard and loved his position. But he was a low-key guy in a large organization that prized sales acumen. He knew his passivity was a problem, so he worked long hours and took on projects his fellow workers would not touch.

She complained long and hard about his work hours. When he was promoted to middle management, she blasted him for all the time he spent away from home. She was incensed that he left little time for family vacations or attending his children's extracurricular activities.

What on earth was she talking about, that she's lonely? She loved her part-time job at the city library and was always busy with the other parents at their children's school. He figured she wanted it all, a fancy lifestyle and a husband who was home when she needed him.

One day, he was going through a stack of papers in one of her desk drawers when he found the letter. From its contents, he could tell she was having an affair with another parent from their children's school.

When he confronted her, she began to cry. He felt angry and guilty at the same time. Angry because she had cheated on him, guilty because he knew he was partly to blame for the affair. Maybe he should have listened when she complained about being lonely, but that still didn't give her the right to step out on him.

Within a few days, he was really angry. He moved out of their home and into an apartment. He asked the company lawyer to recommend an attorney. The whole thing was so disturbing that it took another week for him to call that family lawyer. During the initial interview, he told the lawyer about his broken marriage. He didn't want revenge. He just wanted out of the marriage without harming his children any more than necessary.

The attorney told him the divorce was fairly simple. As much as 75% of their estate was tied up in his 401(k), and so he would have to share it with her. He was surprised. He never imagined she could take part of his retirement. He was the one who worked to set up the account. She knew nothing about it. She never even asked about their retirement.

The more he thought about his cheating wife taking half of his 401(k), the angrier he got. It was his hard-earned money that contributed to the account. How could she possibly ask for a dime of that money? He took good care of her, providing a nice home and comfortable lifestyle.

She said at first the marriage was fine. She focused her attention on their home and the kids while he went to work. But over time, she saw less and less of him. She didn't go looking for the affair. It just happened. She was lonely and desperately wanted someone to pay attention to her. The children were growing up and didn't need her as much. She felt useless and unwanted and a little bit dead inside.

That's when she began to see one of the other fathers. He made her feel wanted and needed again. She thought she had safely hidden all of the letters, but when he found one, she knew the marriage was over. She called her sister, who had just been through her own divorce. She gave her the name of an attorney and she set up a meeting. She told the lawyer up front that the breakup was primarily her fault, but years of neglect had led her to stray.

The lawyer asked her to list her goals. At the top of the list, she mentioned taking care of their children and making sure she was not penniless. After 15 years of part-time work, she didn't know her chances of finding a decent full-time job.

The lawyer told her to go home and make a detailed inventory of their assets. Later that night, she sat in the study, looking through the drawers of financial records. She paid some of the bills, but he took care of all the other financial matters. She found statements from their bank accounts. Then she found the statements for his 401(k). She didn't remember him talking about opening this account. As she thumbed through the paperwork, she realized this was the family's largest asset. If she could get her hands on some of that money, she wouldn't have to worry about finding a job right away.

<u>The result</u> was a divorce where both sides felt partly to blame. This allowed them to display the civility necessary to meet face to face in settlement negotiations.

He just wanted the whole mess behind him. He worked hard to build up his retirement account and didn't want to see it disappear in a divorce settlement. He worked with his lawyer before their first settlement conference to come up with offers that left the retirement account intact. When the time came, he agreed to sell their home and give her the equity. It was enough money for her to live on for the next several years. She also received most of the home furnishings and their best automobile.

When divorcing parties divide a retirement account, the parties enter a Qualified Domestic Relations Order (QDRO) that allows the division and protects the plan member from having to pay taxes on the portion that goes to the nonmember.

To satisfy his need to maintain control over the 401(k) account, instead of using a QDRO he offered to pay her quarterly payments equal to her portion of the retirement account. But his proposal made her an unsecured creditor having to depend largely on his salary to make the payments. Moreover, she would be unable to roll these installment payments over into an IRA or another tax-qualified plan.

Finally, he was persuaded that using a QDRO to divide the 401(k) account could be a "win/win" for both parties. He was relieved of the responsibility to make any payments to her and deal with tax consequences from her portion of the account. In turn, she did not have to depend on him to make quarterly payments and retained the ability to complete a tax-free rollover of an IRA or other tax-qualified plan.

CHAPTER 18

DIVORCES AT A CERTAIN AGE

"ONE WOMAN IN HER 60s, who had been married for 35 years, was an emotional basket case," remembers advisor Dodee Crockett. "Her son kept grilling me with questions while the woman just sat there. I finally said to the son, 'You need to realize that your mother is at a point in her life that when she walks out the front door of her house, she does not know if the ground will be stable under her feet. That is how dramatically her life has changed.'

"And just then the woman started crying, because she had been trying to make her son understand that the financial and emotional issues are all interconnected. She lived her life believing she would die with this person who was now divorcing her. Many people live being one half of something they believe is as solid as bedrock.

"There are more emotional issues the longer you are married, and people really need help establishing and affirming an identity at that point in their lives. Then they can concentrate on finances."

Texas divorces that happen late in life are not statutorily different from others, but the specific facts of each case make them unique. While the overall divorce rate is in a slow decline, older Americans in increasing numbers are heading for divorce court. The number of divorced people in this country over age 65 has nearly doubled since 1980, according to a Temple University study. U.S. Census Bureau statistics show that in 2000, 149,530 Texas women over 60 years of age were divorced, along with 94,370 men.

"The longer the parties are married, the more difficult these cases become," says Crockett. She counsels many people who are married for three decades or more before getting a divorce. Her clients in these cases are most often the wives who stayed at home to raise children while their husbands flourished in their careers.

Divorces after 30 years of marriage or between people age 60 and older are almost exclusively about the distribution of community property. Few of these cases involve child support or visitation schedules because children usually are grown and have their own families.

"In most of these divorces," Crockett explains, "the women are most concerned about staying in their home and the men want to make sure they are able to retire comfortably."

She says the women in these situations have few career assets. That doesn't just include income, pensions or bonus plans. They may not have ever worked outside the home, and they have no idea what they should do and how to prepare for it. An advisor in this instance must help the person project the cash flow available on assets she may take away from the marriage, including equity on real estate holdings, her spouse's retirement funds, defined benefit plans, stock options and bonuses.

The husband may look at his life and conclude that he's provided enough for this woman over the years. He may believe those assets are his because he worked while she stayed home all that time. With such different mindsets, settlement can be difficult.

Financial planners typically believe that you need 70 to 80% of your pre-retirement income to be comfortable after you retire, but that varies with different income levels. Those in the lowest levels, who often live paycheck to paycheck, usually need 100% of pre-retirement income just to pay bills. Crockett says those at the top income levels are locked into the need for disposable income. "They believe many of the luxuries they have are necessities, so they are not happy without them." Middle-class people who divorce late in life seem to adjust better. They have enough money to cover basic needs and the ability to accommodate variations in income.

"But there are personal issues everyone needs to address, so they don't find themselves in a financial quandary," says Crockett. "Like health issues. I suggest the person have a physical. If something is wrong, it's helpful to know before the divorce settlement is finalized. The worst thing that can happen is your divorce is final and six months later you find that you have some terrible illness that's going to be costly and require you to sell your assets at fire sale prices. No one wants to be sick and out of money."

Social Security Benefits

"For people living on social security, a divorce can be horrendous," says Crockett. "It can be a real disaster, because if people don't live together anymore and they each have their social security and not a lot of assets, then you need to look closely at their financial ability to separate and survive."

Attorneys sometimes ask Crockett to evaluate such circumstances and tell them whether couples can survive a breakup or whether the couple should make one last attempt to reconcile. Social Security Administration rules allow a former spouse to receive a benefit based on the other spouse's earning record, even though they are divorced.

The former spouse of an individual entitled to social security retirement or disability benefits may receive benefits if he or she was married to that spouse for 10 years, is at least 62 years old, has not remarried and is not entitled to full benefits on his or her own work record.

These benefits are mostly available to those spouses who stayed home or worked part-time or for short intervals while the other party worked full-time. There are many rules about the collection of social security benefits. They are payable as soon as the recipient spouse is eligible, even if the other spouse does not actually collect benefits at that time. The spouse who collects dependent benefits forfeits the right to them if he or she remarries.

An individual paying into social security can begin to receive benefits at age 62. Many spouses nearing retirement age fail to realize they can receive social security or a portion of their spouse's benefits in the future.

To determine the available benefits under social security, contact the local Social Security Administration office and ask for a printout of benefits available in the future, either individually or through the other spouse. The Social Security Administration can also be contacted on the internet at www.ssa.gov. The Social Security Information Request Form can be obtained online or from your local social security office.

HE SAID
SHE SAID: The Ultimate Loss of Identity

<u>He said</u> that when they married in 1964, she was perfect for him—tall, blond and adventurous. But somewhere between raising children and balancing work, whatever they felt for each other died. He worked long hours to support his new family, and she devoted herself to maintaining the home. He recalled taking her to the hospital, but after that, he just remembers looking up at the dinner table and realizing that his five children were in high school and college.

His job selling employee benefit plans to small companies kept him away from home a lot. When he was home, he just wanted to listen to his stereo and read a book.

Gradually, the children left home. He was surprised how sad it made her, because he thought it was normal.

Shortly after their 40th anniversary, she announced that she wanted a divorce. He didn't know what to think. How long had she been unhappy? When did she stop loving him? He never stopped loving her. He always worked hard to provide for his family. Now she was leaving, explaining that she needed to find herself before it was too late. He didn't know what that meant, but he had no other choice than to let her go.

<u>She said</u> her married life had been nothing but trying to make him happy. It was tough when he never said he loved her or acknowledged that she was doing a good job. At first she thought it was her. Raising five children and taking care

of the family home was sometimes more than she could handle. But she never counted on him for help. He was like an uninvited guest that slept in her bed at night.

To mask her loneliness, she devoted herself to the well-being of her children. It was hard to watch them leave home, partly because it moved her one step closer to being alone with him.

By the time their youngest child left, she filled her days caring for her grandchildren and volunteering two days a week at the church. She dreaded the evenings at home with him. He was not interested in talking to her. After several months of volunteering in the church office, she was offered a full-time position. She accepted, feeling a sense of independence for the first time in decades.

He thought it was the passing of their 40th anniversary that made her want the divorce. It wasn't.

It was actually the celebration of her 60th birthday. She felt trapped in a loveless marriage for her entire adult life. It was her turn to live. The only way she could see obtaining this happiness was to leave him and start a new life for herself.

The result was a divorce that quietly separated two people who had always been apart. He didn't know why she needed or wanted the divorce. He said people their age didn't get divorced, but she was determined.

She was ready to live as a free and independent woman. But she could tell that the divorce upset him greatly. She never meant to hurt him, but she had fallen out of love with him years ago.

After 40 years of marriage, they had their home, two cars, some antique furniture, two flexible premium insurance policies, two burial plots, a couple of small retirement accounts and many frequent flyer miles. This appeared to be their complete estate, until she told her attorney what he did for a living. The attorney found a treasure trove of residuals, the commissions companies pay brokers each time their customers pay their premiums for a new period. In many cases, the sale of insurance policies or benefit plans can produce residual income indefinitely. He didn't reveal these assets because he honestly believed that since he went out and earned the commissions himself and they were in his name, she was not eligible to own them. But all income earned during the marriage and all property purchased with that income are community assets, and they all go into a pot to be divided by the parties.

They submitted their property situation to mediation. Using this method, this late-in-life divorce was settled at a fraction of the cost of going to court. Since she didn't want the house, he kept it, along with some of the furniture, his car and his insurance policy. If she didn't want to live with him, she surely didn't want to stay with him through eternity, so she left him the burial plots. She took her car, the rest of the furniture, her insurance policy, a portion of his retirement money and most of the frequent flyer miles. (Her children were now all over the country and she wanted to visit them.) She also took a stake in his residual income.

Before they celebrated their 41st wedding anniversary, their divorce was final.

CHAPTER 19

Community Debt and the Impact of Bankruptcy

A COMMUNITY ESTATE includes community property but it also includes community debt. The payment of these debts must be addressed in the settlement agreement, noting specifically how certain debts will be divided.

Whenever possible, the two parties together should work diligently to pay off major debts as part of the divorce settlement. This can be done with available funds or by selling assets such as the home, other real estate or personal items. If there isn't enough money available to pay the debts, the settlement agreement should specify which debts each party must pay after the divorce is final.

For each debt, the responsible party should be required to indemnify the other from any loss resulting from the indebtedness, including attorney's fees for enforcement of the obligation. An indemnity is a promise to stand good for an obligation and cover any expenses incurred by the other party related to the debt.

Cataloguing Your Debt

Ignorance of a debt does not excuse you from paying it. Some spouses incur joint debt without their spouse's knowledge, and this should be addressed before resolution of the divorce. But parties who use a joint credit card can't really say they didn't know about the debt.

A good source of information about debts you might not know about is a credit bureau report. You may be amazed to find the number of debts listed in your name.

Unless you make an exhaustive review of your credit history, never sign a settlement agreement that says each of the parties will pay the debts listed in each of their names. You may be shocked when numerous finance companies call on you for payment of debts incurred by your spouse.

Apportioning Debt

Whether you agree to split up the debt or the court orders it, several factors determine responsibility for a debt, including the following:

- Who retains any asset securing the debt after the divorce
- Purpose of the debt
- Financial prospects of the parties now and in the future
- Any agreement between the parties concerning the debts
- Overall apportionment of property
- Length of the marriage
- Fault of the parties

Provide your attorney with a list of all debts, including a breakdown of who incurred which debts. Also, provide a detailed list of purchases made on an account and the current status of those assets. This information should also include the name and address of creditors, as well as account numbers.

Which Debts Belong to Whom?

Ambiguity is one of the most vexing problems when dividing assets or debts. The settlement agreement cannot merely say that the parties have certain debts, the largest ones will be paid off from the sale of assets and the parties shall split the others. The agreement must be specific about the particular debts and their amounts.

It may be a good idea to pay off as many debts as possible, cancel the accounts or convert them into the name of one spouse during the divorce. You can also specify in the settlement agreement that certain debts be refinanced within a certain time to remove your name from the obligation, since we already know that an order of the family court in Texas cannot remove your liability for a debt even if your spouse has agreed to be responsible for it. It is important to note that this is only possible when the other spouse qualifies for refinancing.

An irresponsible spouse can often blemish the other's credit rating during and after the divorce and this possibility should be taken into consideration in the settlement negotiations. To reach a settlement, parties may agree to divide the joint debts in some manner. The attorneys should include language in the agreement that the party responsible for a debt indemnifies and holds the other party harmless for the debt.

When there are few assets or the incomes of the parties are nearly equal, the parties may share the debt load. In such cases, each party may make payments to specific creditors while trying to sell an asset (the marital residence, for example) and use the proceeds from that sale to reduce or pay off joint debt.

Bankruptcy and its Effect on Community Debts

Personal bankruptcy filings in the United States jumped 40% in 2007 due to rising mortgage payments, unemployment and other pressures. The increase followed a sharp decline from a year earlier, when a new law made it more difficult for consumers to seek bankruptcy-court protection from creditors.

"People generally file for bankruptcy because of illness, loss of a job, some other temporary setback, excessive use of credit cards and divorce," says Michelle Mendez, bankruptcy attorney with Hunton Williams in Dallas.

And while bankruptcy may be more difficult to obtain, it still often goes hand in hand with divorce because there may not be enough money to pay the community debts or one spouse may decide to use bankruptcy as a weapon against the other.

The threat of bankruptcy is always serious as it relates to community assets and debts. The divorce agreement may state that one spouse is responsible for certain debts. The agreement may say the paying spouse holds the other party harmless and is responsible for any and all obligations of the debt. But the filing of a bankruptcy petition after divorce can create havoc and the specific terms of the agreement become very critical.

Under the new law, bankruptcy filers who have money cannot simply avoid paying off debts. But the debts can still be greatly reduced, leaving more money for the payment of ongoing expenses, including support; taxes can be paid, without interest; and the divorce can be simplified by reducing much of the community debt.

The situation gets more complicated when one party surprises the other by filing alone. Then the legal worlds of state family law and federal bankruptcy law collide, and the bankruptcy courts are left to sift through the wreckage. A bankruptcy filing pulls all the community property into the bankruptcy estate. Such a move changes everything, assuring that the available assets will be used immediately to pay debts and reducing flexibility in handling the assets and debts of the marriage.

Fortunately, the bankruptcy code attempts to protect the rights of children and former spouses by specifying that support —whether child support or alimony—is not dischargeable in bankruptcy. These payments are priority claims that must be paid before unsecured creditors and taxes.

"If your spouse files a bankruptcy petition and there are obligations to pay, you can lose rights if you fail to object quickly," says Mendez. She has seen many settlement agreements fall apart at the last minute because one party simply decided against giving the other party some property and, instead, declared bankruptcy.

"Sometimes an ex-spouse or a soon-to-be ex files for bankruptcy figuring they will cause the other party to just give up," says Mendez. "This is a time when you need knowledgeable and watchful counsel to protect your rights. Given the financial peril that divorce creates, it's hard to believe that people risk manipulating the system like they do. That really is fraught with peril. I have never seen anyone win a divorce with a bankruptcy."

Alternatives to Bankruptcy

In a perfect world, the available resources would be enough to pay all the bills each month. But the world is not perfect or people wouldn't divorce. Dividing a household that was barely meeting obligations into two single-income households with comparable expenses can quickly lead to a startling realization: despite all best efforts, the means do not meet the ends. Calls from creditors or their collection agents cause people to consider bankruptcy. But there are many alternatives to bankruptcy that can save a person's credit rating and help them regain control of their monthly expenses, including the following:

Home equity line of credit — Real property tends to appreciate in value. A common source of money to pay off debts is a home equity line of credit. Most are available for up to 80% of a home's value, and in some cases the interest is tax deductible.

Renegotiate secured loans — Loans secured by homes and automobiles are often the largest debts, and bankruptcy does not wipe them out. Sometimes you can negotiate a lower interest rate on a home loan refinancing and save several hundred dollars each month. If the lender will not cooperate, it may be possible to refinance the loan elsewhere, extend the loan over a longer period and reduce the payments.

Renegotiate unsecured loans — Lenders realize that bankruptcy can severely affect unsecured loans, so they are more eager to compromise. Some merchants will reduce or eliminate interest or carrying charges to recover the principal.

Defer the debt — With unsecured loans, such as revolving charge accounts, the creditor may allow a grace period in order to keep a good customer and recover the money.

Interest reduction — Creditors may not be willing to reduce the principal, but will reduce the interest on a loan.

Debt consolidation — Some traditional lenders offer loans to consolidate debts into one manageable payment at a reasonable interest rate. Talk with a personal banker for additional information. Avoid transferring balances between credit cards. While many cards offer teaser rates to induce such transfers, consumers often get caught rolling the debt between cards, incurring unnecessary finance and interest charges and managing an ever-increasing debt load.

Credit counseling — These agencies provide an additional alternative when traditional lending options are not available. The Consumer Credit Counseling Service (CCCS), with offices throughout Texas, sponsors a debt management program to repay debts by restructuring a budget and negotiating with creditors. CCCS is a nonprofit organization dedicated to helping people solve credit issues.

Creditors often reduce interest and finance charges for CCCS program participants. The one monthly payment is typically less than payments to individual creditors. Plans can pay off obligations in as little as three years, a substantially shorter time than making the minimum monthly payment on the same obligations.

Part Three
LOOK TO THE FUTURE

HE SAID
SHE SAID: No Clear Line Between
Child Support and Visitation

He said he wasn't the best husband, but he'd been a good father and didn't deserve to be punished. When she took their kids and left him, she had to know times would be tough. Providing for them when they were together was never easy. From his work as a finish carpenter, how was he supposed to pay child support and have anything left to live on?

They fought from day one. If it wasn't about the kids, she was annoyed that he was broke, that he stayed out drinking late at night or that he didn't help out enough around the house.

After four years of misery, she told him she was moving out. That was fine with him. Now he could see his kids when he wanted and didn't have to worry about the day-to-day hassles.

In the divorce settlement, they agreed to joint custody. Still, the kids lived with her most of the time. He paid child support and had visitation rights. His child support was not as much as the Texas child support guidelines required, but they agreed to equally split certain expenses for the children that included day care and after-school care, extracurricular activities and medical expenses. She sent him an itemized list at the end of each month, outlining the child support obligations they agreed to pay. She went ahead and paid these expenses and he reimbursed her for his part. At first, he sent the money every month. But he had a few other priorities for his money, and since she was already paying for everything, he figured the basics would be covered even if he didn't contribute.

He tried to keep the visitation schedule they agreed upon, but after an on-the-job accident left him unable to pay child support for a couple of months, she refused to give him time with the kids. He was frustrated with the situation and felt left out of their lives.

He began to vent his frustrations with coworkers. One of the men suggested contacting a lawyer. He didn't want to take this route, but if it meant he would get to see his children more, it was worth it. After his first meeting with the family law attorney, he came to the conclusion that his only hope was to take his ex-wife to court.

She said that giving birth to their son changed her life forever. She'd just been a good-time girl before that, but now she was ready to get serious. And after their daughter was born, she began to see that his wild ways and his lack of ambition would always bother her.

After trying to make it work, she gave up and moved into an apartment that was barely big enough for her and the kids. Initially, she thought her job would be enough to support them. She didn't know two children could cost so much. Each month, she worried herself sick and waited until she was desperate for money before calling him. She hated having to do it. He was always eager to see the kids, but he rarely paid her the child support he owed and was always full of excuses.

How could he be comfortable with his children when he wouldn't provide for them? When he visited them, she said if he couldn't provide for them, he had no right to see them.

<u>The result</u> was a court battle over child support and visitation. The judge slammed him for spending much of his money on good times and too little on his children. He was held in contempt of court for failing to pay child support in a timely fashion. She felt pretty good hearing all of this, until the judge held her in contempt for denying him visitation. Both child support and visitation are vital matters. But they are completely independent and one doesn't depend on the other.

The judge ordered him to pay a specific amount of child support each month and let it be known that she could not restrict his access to the children.

CHAPTER 20

SUPPORT YOUR CHILDREN

PAYING CHILD SUPPORT is one of the best ways divorced parents can tell children that even though the family is not together, they are still loved. Unfortunately, child support is the debt most often left unpaid. In Texas alone, 1,088,020 children were owed $9.3 billion in 2003 that was never paid.

Over the entire country, more than $100 billion in child support was unpaid to 18 million children that same year, and that number represents only one-half of the support ordered. The federal government estimates that if all child support was paid, there would be almost no children living in poverty in this country.

Of course, some child support goes unpaid for legitimate reasons, because those obligated to pay it have lost jobs or suffer from a wide range of physical or mental problems that keep them from earning enough money. But the vast majority of what we've come to call "deadbeat parents" simply refuse to pay their obligations, choosing to remain purposely underemployed, spend money on themselves, or support their new families instead.

"For many kids, child support payments are the only measure they have of love from an estranged parent," says Dr. Maryanne Watson. "If the parent at least continues to support them financially, even when they don't support them emotionally, it is parental participation. When a parent abandons them emotionally and financially, it's a double blow."

Child Support Collection

Powerful forces are working against deadbeat parents. The federal government has created the Parent Locator Service to harness the resources of the Social Security Administration and the Internal Revenue Service to locate a nonpaying parent or his or her employer.

Once the parent is found, the custodial parent can enforce a child support order signed by the judge and collect unpaid support. The law also permits the IRS to pay child support arrears from tax refunds the nonpaying parent may be owed by the government.

In Texas, the Attorney General's office is responsible for collections on a state level. Check the government listings in your telephone directory for the local Attorney General's office. A number of private companies will collect child support for a percentage of the money recovered. Use these companies only if government sources fail to collect, since they take a percentage and that reduces the amount collected. And pay no fees in advance.

The Yellow Pages lists companies under Child Support Collections that can help you enforce child support obligations or you can retain a private attorney.

Calculating Child Support

The amount of child support you must pay is calculated by child support guidelines contained in the Texas Family Code. The charts that accompany the guidelines are updated each year. Under the court order, the parent required to pay child support is called the obligor, while the parent who receives support is the obligee.

Child support is figured by multiplying the proper percentage by the obligor parent's net income. You begin with gross income, which consists of salary, commissions, overtime pay, tips, bonuses, interest, dividends, rental income, royalty income, trust income, retirement income, disability income and any other form of income. In 2009, the Texas Legislature clarified that money received from federal public assistance programs, Temporary Assistance for Needy Families or for care of foster children was not included. The amount of monthly resources subject to child support is capped at $7,500.

From gross income you subtract social security taxes, federal income tax (based on the tax rate for a single person claiming one exemption), union dues and health insurance premiums for the children.

Once you calculate the net monthly resources, you pay a percentage of those resources as follows:

1 child	20% of net resources
2 children	25% of net resources
3 children	30% of net resources
4 children	35% of net resources

5 children   40% of net resources

6+ children   Not less than the amount for 5 children

Under the Texas Child Support Guidelines, here is an example showing what an obligor parent pays for two children living with the same mother, not counting his deduction for health insurance payments:

$4,500.00	Gross monthly income
– 1,031.75	Taxes
$3,468.25	Net income
x 25%	Percentage for two children
$867.06	Monthly child support under the guidelines

These numbers are slightly different for children from two different marriages. A father with an obligation to support two children with different mothers will pay 17.5% of net earnings for each child instead of 25% for children living in the same household.

Special Circumstances

Divorcing parties with high incomes and numerous assets, or those who share almost equal access to the children, often follow different rules from those described above.

As we stated earlier, the child support guidelines apply only to the first $7,500 of net income. When the parent earns more, the court can look at the income and assets of the parties, and the needs of the child, to determine if additional child support should be paid.

If a child is disabled and has extraordinary needs, the court may deviate from the guidelines to ensure that the child gets the additional services he or she needs.

Another common variable is the amount of possession shared by the parents. If the parents have substantially equal assets and net resources and the children alternate living one week with one parent and one with the other, the guidelines may not be right for the situation.

Often in this situation, courts will consider the offsetting of child support between the parties. For examplr, the court will calculate the child support that would be owed by each party based in individual income. The court then subtracts the lower amount from the higher amount to arrive at the child support net amount owed by the higher wage earner. If party one owes $500 per month in support and party two owes $200 per month, then party one is to pay $300 per month to party two.

That doesn't mean child support payments should be linked to how much visitation a parent receives. A parent who should receive child support cannot deny visitation because an obligor parent fails to pay support payments. And an obligor parent cannot withhold child support due to visitation problems. Even though these situations are prohibited in Texas, vindictiveness, petty behavior and ignorance allow them to happen. It's a pity, but sometimes parents risk contempt of court and a night in jail in their zeal to use the children to get even with an ex-spouse.

Pay Child Support through State System

Child support is often subject to side deals and negotiation, but it is too important to leave to an informal collection system. Child support is for the children, not for the custodial parent. Texas law requires that it be paid in nearly every case. To avoid disruption or additional legal problems, follow the rules and make certain the correct amount is paid in the right manner.

The Texas Family Code provides for child support payments to be sent to the state disbursement unit in San Antonio and this state government agency forwards the payments to recipient parents. Payments can no longer be made directly between the two parties.

In addition, many child support orders include a wage withholding order. The paying parent's employer is ordered to withhold child support from that parent's paycheck and send it through the state system.

How Long Do You Pay Child Support?

Under the Texas Family Code, the court may order either or both parents to support children until:

- The child is 18 years of age or graduates from high school, as long as the child is fully enrolled in school;
- The child is married or has his or her minority removed by law;
- The child dies; or
- In the case of a child who is physically or mentally disabled, indefinitely.

In Texas, however, college expenses cannot be ordered by the court and must be agreed to as part of the divorce settlement if they are included in the decree. Many Texas parents agree to pay these expenses or divide them between the parties. These expenses may include tuition, books and room and board. The parties may also agree to pay a weekly allowance, fees, fraternity and sorority expenses and transportation to and from school. But unless the parents agree to such a provision, the court cannot require a parent to pay for these items. If, for example, a child wants to attend a private university, the agreement should specify the anticipated expenses minus any scholarships or grants.

A parent ordered to pay child support for two children does not have that amount cut in half when one child reaches age 18. For example, if the decree orders child support of $750 per month for two children, support is not reduced to $375 for the youngest child when the older one reaches majority. Instead, the guidelines determine the amount. For the remaining child, the amount is reduced from 25% to 20% of net resources.

CHAPTER 21

Insuring Your Health and Life

AT THIS WRITING, 25.1% of all Texans are without health insurance, the highest percentage of uninsured of any state in the country. If both parties to a Texas divorce work and their employers offer health coverage, they may escape being one of the uninsured. If one party does not work, works for an employer who offers no coverage or is covered by the spouse's insurance during the marriage, this issue needs to be closely addressed in the settlement agreement.

Health Insurance for the Children

Texas has 1.4 million children without health insurance, for the past decade the highest number of any state in the country. A large proportion of uninsured Texas children are from moderate-income families. Many go without coverage because parents who are obligated to provide insurance fail to comply with a court order.

The parent obligated to pay child support is required to provide major medical insurance for a minor child. That obligation may be continued by agreement until the child graduates from college. In most cases, health insurance is available through the obligated spouse's employment.

When that spouse does not have coverage in this manner, he or she may pursue the purchase of it for the child in one of the following ways:

- Reimburse the obligee spouse for providing coverage for the child on his or her employee policy.
- Enroll the child in the state Children's Health Insurance Program, if incomes qualify you for it.
- If the child attends a private school or is in college, you can buy into group policies at many of these schools.
- For people under the poverty level, apply for Medicaid insurance.
- Purchase an individual policy, although this is the most expensive way to provide coverage.

If a parent must provide health insurance and fails to do that, he or she may be obligated to pay all medical expenses if the child becomes ill or is injured. The question of who pays medical expenses above and beyond what's covered by health insurance should be answered in the settlement agreement. If health insurance is not available due to preexisting conditions or other factors, the obligor parent might still be liable for the total expenses of an illness or injury. Even when the child is fully covered, there are expenses including the deductible, copayments or other extraordinary charges for doctors, hospitals, labs, prescription drugs, optical, dental, orthodontic or other medically related expenses.

If a child is diagnosed with a major illness, these expenses can be devastating and could force a parent into bankruptcy or long-term debt.

Health Insurance for Your Spouse

Most health insurance plans will not allow one spouse to provide coverage for the other after the divorce. A spouse needing coverage often can look to the following options:

Coverage through an employer — The spouse may not have selected this coverage before the divorce because it isn't the best coverage or it may be at a high price, but it is available and usually is more affordable than other alternatives.

COBRA (Consolidated Omnibus Budget Reconciliation Act of 1985) — If an employer plan discontinues coverage, this federal program provides coverage for a limited time. The plan is administered through the employer and should offer the same benefits as the employer plan at a slightly higher premium. Each spouse should confirm that this coverage is available before final resolution of the case.

Individual plan — A spouse who is relatively young and in good physical condition may qualify for an individual policy sold by a company representative or insurance broker. Usually these policies are more expensive and offer less coverage than group plans.

State risk pool — Texas offers health insurance for people who cannot obtain coverage because of preexisting conditions or other factors. The plan is highly restrictive and usually has a long waiting list.

If one spouse has a major preexisting condition such as cancer or heart trouble, this condition may not be covered by the new insurance following the divorce. This possibility should be examined to assess the costs associated with medical care.

Cancer or other major illnesses can play a large role in a party's financial need due to the associated costs, as well as limitations such an illness may place on the spouse's ability to earn a living. As a result, parties may wind up disputing the severity of health conditions due to the potential implications.

For instance, the spouse obligated to pay child support may claim an on-the-job back injury, restricting work and the payment of child support. The other spouse may deny the injury, claiming an attempt to escape responsibility.

The obligated spouse's attorney may have to hire a physician to assess the situation. Expert medical witnesses are expensive. Such an investment is worthwhile only when a large amount of money is at stake. The spouse could significantly reduce the cost of such a move by getting all medical records related to the condition for the lawyer to review. Otherwise, the lawyer may have to subpoena the medical records at considerable expense.

Life Insurance Protects Future Payments

Certified financial planner Mike Jarvis of Dallas says that whenever child support or other payments over time are part of a divorce settlement, insurance should be required on the life of the spouse who will be making the payments. In fact, insuring the lives of both parents makes perfect sense. In most cases, when a custodial parent dies, the noncustodial parent takes on the responsibility for children and an increasing financial burden.

"If you are a spouse taking care of three kids," Jarvis says, "and you need $2,500 a month to cover their expenses, that's $30,000 a year. You need to know that if your ex-spouse dies, you can replace that income. This may sound cold-blooded, but if a parent dies the children keep living and spending."

Many parties agree that the obligor spouse should maintain a life insurance policy to cover support payments until all debts are paid. The obligated spouse can be required to maintain a life insurance policy for a specified dollar amount, for a certain time period, and name the spouse or children as beneficiaries while there is a financial obligation under the divorce agreement.

Protection for children, if one parent should die, is essential to a successful divorce. The settlement agreement should specify that the obligated spouse cannot modify the life insurance policies or reduce their value by borrowing against them. Provisions for complying with life insurance requirements can be included in the decree, such as requiring the obligor spouse to provide periodic proof of coverage as well as authorizing the payee spouse to contact the insurance company directly to obtain this information.

The best way to make certain insurance is not dropped or otherwise misused is to negotiate ownership of the policy and how payments are made. "If the payor spouse owns the policy," Jarvis explains, "that spouse may remarry. Then he or she has the ability down the road, if you don't own the contract, to change the beneficiary. We see this often, when the beneficiary is revocable. It's easier when you simply own the policy from the start."

Provisions for establishment of a trust may also be included in the decree. Under such a trust, the obligated spouse specifies a trustee—often the former spouse or a family member— who is required to use life insurance proceeds for the benefit of each child. When the children reach majority, the trustee usually distributes any money remaining in the trust.

"This is an often overlooked issue," Jarvis says. "People overlook insurance when they are married. They certainly overlook it as they are divorcing. It's not required by law, but it's a perfectly sensible thing to have."

HE SAID
SHE SAID: Helping Her Regain Her Balance

<u>She said</u> she never had any intention of staying home after the birth of their first child. He pushed for the idea. There were so many reasons for her to continue working and only one reason to stay home. She agonized over the decision for months. But in the end, she decided to leave her job.

Staying home presented a difficult transition. Her days were filled with household chores, chasing after her son and making sure dinner was ready when he got home. She was lonely. She began to cling to him as her only portal to the outside world. He seemed so unsympathetic to her needs and her growing depression.

On several occasions, she approached him about returning to work. He would not consider the idea. Her place was at home.

They began to argue. The argument mostly revolved around money. She was never allowed to see the family checkbook. He only told her whether or not she exceeded her weekly budget.

He turned into a controlling person. They never talked anymore, never spent time together as a couple. She felt her marriage slipping away. She quietly began to collect financial information and contacted an attorney. She wanted out.

After years of staying home, she knew that her earning capacity had diminished. She told her attorney that alimony was not a mere option in her case; it was a priority. There was no way she could get back on her feet without it.

<u>He said</u> he was excited when the baby came. He always wanted a son. But he was adamant that a stranger would not raise his child. She would have to stay home. Carrying the weight of the family was stressful, and she didn't help the situation. She complained constantly about being lonely. He was frustrated listening to her whine. She didn't realize what a privilege it was for her to stay home. Other women had to balance so much in their lives. All she had to do was take care of one child and keep the house clean.

He gave her a generous weekly allowance, but somehow each week she spent more. Life is filled with trade-offs, and she couldn't spend money like she did when she had a job. Her answer to the problem was to return to work.

She refused to see his point of view on this subject. He could not understand why it was so difficult for her. Her depression affected every facet of their marriage. He was seriously thinking about separating to see if she would come to her senses.

When he suggested the idea, she agreed and told him she had already been speaking to an attorney about a divorce. He felt betrayed.

<u>The result</u> was a separation and divorce marred by accusations. She called him controlling for keeping her at home. He said she was unappreciative of the freedom he allowed her. They agreed on joint custody of their son. They split their personal property easily enough, but the division of other assets, mostly their home and his retirement account, was more difficult. It shouldn't have been, since their needs and

wants worked hand in hand. She was concerned about her future. Over the time she spent at home, her job skills eroded and technology passed her by. To earn enough money, she needed additional training at a vocational school or local college.

He decided that one of them needed to stay in their home, for their son. He was the one who could afford it, but he couldn't stay there if he had to give her half the home equity and half of his retirement account.

So he lived in their home and they worked out a plan that included him giving her rehabilitative alimony of $2,500 a month for three years in addition to child support. She used the money to move into an apartment and start back to school.

CHAPTER 22

ALIMONY AND MAINTENANCE

YES, ALIMONY IS AWARDED in Texas. Will you receive alimony after your Texas divorce? Probably not. The Texas Legislature enacted an alimony statute in 1995, but it is one of the most restrictive statutes on this subject in the nation. The law is written so narrowly that most people fail to qualify.

The statute specifically provides that alimony is not warranted unless the spouse seeking maintenance has diligently tried to seek suitable employment or develop the necessary skills to become self-supporting during the couple's separation period.

Limited Eligibility

Under the Texas Family Code, alimony is intended as a stop-gap measure for a divorced spouse (usually the wife) who was out of the job market for many years, lacks job skills and does not have enough assets to support herself and her children. At its best, alimony in Texas is rehabilitative in nature, allowing one spouse to become trained for a career. If you have no assets and no skills, and have been married for at least 10 years, you may be entitled to alimony for a period not to exceed three years (or indefinitely in case of a disability), up to a maximum of $2,500 per month or 20% of the ex-spouse's average monthly gross income. The problem is that most spouses in marriages with assets don't qualify for alimony. And those who qualify are often in marriages where the husband does not have the earning capacity to pay much, if any, support.

Types of Alimony

In Texas, there are three basic types of support:

Temporary Spousal Support — This support is ordered by a judge at a temporary hearing as a transitional mechanism while the divorce is pending.

Maintenance — This is usually court-ordered in a divorce decree, but with the restrictions already explained.

Contractual Alimony — This is probably the most common form of alimony. While poor women qualify for alimony more than any other socioeconomic group, middle-class and high-income people actually receive money by agreement rather than a lump-sum payment of the community assets.

Parties may agree to pay alimony to their exes because they worry, for their children's sake, about the other party's ability to handle a large chunk of money all at once. There are also tax advantages to paying alimony and the payor spouse may want to pocket the savings. Sometimes, when the main community asset is a closely held business, the couple will agree to alimony rather than the business owner selling the company or borrowing money to give the other spouse a share of the equity.

Factors to Consider

When a court assesses maintenance, the following factors are considered in determining the nature, amount, duration and manner of periodic payments:

- Financial resources of the receiving spouse
- Education level and employment skills of both spouses
- Length of the marriage
- Age, employment history, earning ability and physical and emotional condition of the receiving spouse
- Financial ability of the paying spouse
- Any financial mismanagement or concealment by spouses
- Comparative financial resources of both spouses
- Contributions to education, training or increased earning power by one spouse to the other
- Property brought to the marriage by either spouse
- Contribution of a spouse as homemaker
- Any marital misconduct of the receiving spouse
- Efforts by the receiving spouse to pursue employment counseling

Modifying Alimony

Although the court cannot modify contractual alimony, court-ordered spousal support may be modified by an order of the court when there has been a "material and substantial" change of circumstances. The evidence presented to the court must be completely new. Any issues addressed previously in the spousal support arrangements are not means for modification.

Here are some of the factors a court considers in a motion to modify support:

- Change in the supporting spouse's income
- Change in the assets available to either party
- Supporting spouse's new responsibilities
- Supporting spouse's physical or mental health
- Change in receiving spouse's rehabilitation schedule

For example, a man is ordered by the court to pay his soon-to-be ex-wife alimony payments of $2,500 per month for three years while she completes a training program in computer technology at a local college. Two years into the agreement, the man's father dies and he becomes the principal caregiver for his mother, who has Alzheimer's disease. In order for him to work and care for his mother, the man hires a nurse to stay with her during the day. The man petitions the court and receives a reduction in support to cover this new expense. The court can never increase the amount of maintenance payments, only reduce them.

Tax Implications

Under the Internal Revenue Code, alimony or spousal maintenance payments are a deduction from the gross income of the payor spouse and are income to the spouse receiving the money. To qualify for alimony tax treatment, alimony or separate maintenance payments must meet the following requirements:
- Payments must be in cash or a cash equivalent.
- Payee must be a spouse or former spouse of the payor.

- Payments must be according to a divorce or separation instrument.
- Instrument must not designate that payments are not to be included in payee's gross income and not allowable as a deduction by the payor.
- Payor and payee must not be living together when alimony payments are made.
- Payments must cease at death of the payee.
- Payment cannot be child support in any form.
- Alimony or separate maintenance payments exceeding $15,000 in either of the first two years must not be front loaded as determined by a specific formula set out in the IRC.
- Payor and payee cannot file a joint tax return.

The IRS provides a penalty for front-end loading of alimony payments. This provision was designed to discourage property divisions disguised as alimony. If the payments made in the first post-separation year exceed the average of the payments made in the second and third years by $15,000 or more, the IRS will hold that the payor spouse made excess payments in the first year. Any excess above $15,000 will be recaptured and added to the obligor's gross income for the third year.

Impact of Bankruptcy

Once again, alimony and child support cannot be discharged in bankruptcy. These are two of only a handful of debt types that must be paid regardless of whether or not a person declares bankruptcy.

Comments from Divorcing People That Make A Family Lawyer Flinch

Ever wonder what comments you can make that cause divorce lawyers to flinch? You might think it is the extremely personal features of life, but to be honest we have heard it all. You can't embarrass us, and nothing can turn us away. There are, however, plenty of financial details that cause us to gasp and roll our eyes, knowing that we must address this in order to move forward. They are show stoppers and deal breakers that can put a divorce off track.

The following is a selection of the comments and the rationales behind them that can give us pause:

"I'll give her $100,000 when the divorce is final, but make it alimony so I can deduct it."

The Internal Revenue Code prohibits disguising a property settlement as contractual alimony. Such alimony cannot be front loaded, but must be spread out more evenly, at least during the first three calendar years.

"I really don't want to spend the money to conduct discovery. I have a pretty good idea that his inventory looks about right."

Don't just assume that you are getting accurate information from your soon-to-be ex-spouse about the values of assets and liabilities. If you fail to use the most often utilized means of discovery — interrogatories, requests for admission, depositions — your estranged mate may be left to interpret values in a way that benefits him or her most. This is especially true with the holdings in a pension plan. You might have seen the tax value and believe you know values, but present-day values may be quite different.

"Get this divorce over now. I just put a contract on a new house."

Here is where the attorney must say, "Slow down, Lone Ranger." Too often, divorcing people get in a hurry and mistakenly create community property when that's not what they intended.

"Don't worry, we've agreed on everything, and we both want to use you as our attorney."

What may seem like a cost-effective way of handling your divorce can turn into a financial nightmare. Under the disciplinary rules of the State Bar of Texas, an attorney cannot represent both sides of the same divorce. Bar rules do allow an attorney to act as an intermediary, mediating issues between people who have no conflicts. Problems arise when a party to a divorce believes his or her rights are being protected by an attorney who is advising both sides, but the attorney knows that he or she represents only one side of the divorce.

"Get me the prenup this afternoon. She'll sign it tonight so we can go ahead with the wedding tomorrow."

Once we had to fight to enforce prenuptial and post-nuptial agreements in Texas. Now the courts usually uphold these agreements and attempts to break the prenup meet with less success. The problem with the statement above is the haste to nail down the prenup. Under the Texas Family Code, a fair and reasonable disclosure of property or financial obligations must be provided. Financial disclosures beyond this must be waived. There just may not be enough time to fulfill all the requirements and get the prenup signed overnight.

CHAPTER 23

Common Tax Issues

TAX ATTORNEY CHARLES BILLINGS believes that no spouse should ever jeopardize his or her tax situation through ignorance.

"But you see something different all the time," says Billings. "Today, with e-filing of income tax returns, one spouse can file without ever getting the signature of the other party. What couples need to do is sit down and discuss the return with a CPA there to explain it. That's not just in case of a divorce, but what if your spouse dies? You want to understand the economics of your family's tax situation."

Before the late 1990s, a spouse who blindly signed the tax return was equally responsible for errors or outright fraud. In 1998, reforms of the Internal Revenue Code exempted certain spouses from payment of tax bills due to the actions of an ex-spouse.

Recently, a Texas case cast a shadow over innocent-spouse relief. In a surprise decision involving a Texas woman, the Tax Court ruled that simply knowing about a tax-return entry or income not reported by a spouse can be enough to remove the presumption of innocence, even if the allegedly innocent spouse had no idea the return was wrong.

The woman admitted knowing her husband took $230,000 from a retirement account and paid off a mortgage, bought an SUV and met other expenses. But when she asked him about the transactions before signing the return, her husband falsely assured her that it was legal to deduct the mortgage payment and reduce the tax on the retirement money. Such rulings are designed to punish spouses who ignore tax laws.

"Spouses frequently attempt to allocate tax deductions or credits between themselves in a divorce agreement," says CPA and family law attorney Jim Wingate. "Most if not all of these attempts are ineffective. For example, couples argue over who gets the deduction for property taxes and mortgage interest paid prior to their divorce and may allocate those deductions to one or the other party. Under the Internal Revenue Code and applicable case law, deductions go to the person reporting the income from which the deductions were paid. Likewise, there is a long list of what are called 'tax attributes' that pass to one party or the other by operation of the Code in spite of the parties' attempts to allocate them."

Prior Year Liabilities or Refund

The settlement agreement should specify which party is responsible for prior year tax liabilities, in the event of a deficiency, or who receives a refund, in the case of an overpayment. Such a provision can protect you even if the error is not discovered until after the divorce. This is especially important when only one spouse operates a business and the other spouse has no idea about the legitimacy of deductions taken by that spouse. Taxpayers filing jointly are each liable for any tax, interest or penalties associated with that return. The agreement should indemnify the spouse who is not responsible, although the IRS will attempt to collect from either party.

Such tax issues are overlooked by a vast majority of divorcing people. The spouse who has the return prepared has a great deal of control over possible refunds. Overpayment of taxes by someone preparing the return has also become a popular way to hide money in a divorce.

Who Files Current Year Tax Return?

While married couples living together typically file joint returns, divorced spouses must file separately, often leading to higher tax brackets and larger tax burdens. Your marital status as of the end of the tax year determines your tax status. If a couple divorces on December 31, they cannot file a joint return for that year. If the tax savings are significant if you wait to divorce, a settlement agreement could be entered into before the end of the year with the divorce decree finalized in January.

One or both spouses may have lower income tax costs from filing as married rather than single. If the divorce is amicable enough to make a delay possible, the spouse with the higher income may consider accelerating income into the current tax year and delaying deductions until the following year. Such a move could lower overall taxes.

Before 2003, divorcing spouses were required by the Internal Revenue Code to report one-half of total community income in each of their respective tax returns in the year of divorce. Divorcing parties frequently ignored this requirement because they did not want to ask their former spouses for this information and many tax preparers did not understand how this provision applied to Texas community property law. Former spouses simply reported their own earnings in their respective returns for the year of divorce.

To legitimize this practice, the Texas Legislature enacted a property statute in 2003 that allows divorcing parties to agree to be responsible just for the taxes on his or her earnings and property under that party's control. This new provision, still unknown to many divorcing people and their advisors, also applies to the prior year in situations where divorce proceedings span two tax years.

Payments and Transfers

Property transfers from one spouse to another in connection with a divorce are nontaxable events. Neither party realizes a gain or loss for income tax purposes when they transfer property between themselves as part of the allocation of assets in their divorce. But there may be future tax consequences from the division of assets. For instance, a couple divorces with only two assets: 500 shares of stock with a current market value of $50,000 and a $50,000 certificate of deposit. Since the CD is a form of cash, its tax basis is always equal to the stated value of the CD because the tax basis of cash is simply the amount of cash.

The tax basis of the stock, on the other hand, may be different from its current value. If the stock appreciates substantially, its tax basis may be much less than its current market value. In our example, if you purchased the stock four months before the parties' divorce for $20,000, you have a potential gain of $30,000 now that it's worth $50,000.

In this example, the party receiving the CD would realize $50,000 from the divorce allocation, but the other party would ultimately realize something less than $50,000 when the stock is sold and taxes paid.

When the parties are in different marginal tax brackets, you might consider transferring marital property with a larger built-in gain to the spouse in the lower tax bracket. You could transfer marital property with little or no gain, or that may have actually declined in value, to the spouse in the higher tax bracket.

Let's say that a divorcing couple has divided much of their property, leaving a lake house and some stocks. The market value of the stock is approximately the same as the equity in the house. Giving one person the stock and the other the house may seem equal, except that the two assets could have widely differing tax bases. Since the husband is retired and in a much lower marginal tax bracket than the wife, who is still working, it might be equitable for the husband to receive the asset with the greater potential tax gain.

Property arrangements are so complex and subject to so many variables that you need to check them out with a tax expert.

Who Gets Dependency Exemptions?

A taxpayer may claim a personal tax exemption for any qualifying dependent, which usually includes all children age 18 and under living at home. The trial court has no authority to award the federal tax dependency exemption to one parent or the other. The dependency exemption is dictated by the Internal Revenue Code, which grants the exemption to the parent having custody of the child for the greater portion of the year, unless the parties agree otherwise.

If the parents agree to equal periods of possession, the decree should specify that one of the spouses file IRS Form 8332 to let the taxman know who gets to claim the kids. If there is more than one child, the parents may agree to divide the dependency exemptions. If there is only one child, the parties may alternate the claim.

When negotiating tax exemptions, make sure you don't waste them. That is possible if they go to a parent with too little or too much income. You must have income from which to deduct the amount of the exemption. Without income, there is no deduction. Similarly, you can waste the child exemption on the rich. For people who make over a certain threshold, which changes each year, personal exemptions begin to phase out and are completely without benefit at a certain amount.

Retirement Plan Issues

As detailed earlier, you can divide a retirement plan as part of the settlement and avoid tax consequences by entering a Qualified Domestic Relations Order (QDRO). A QDRO basically divides one plan into two, leaving a portion in the name of the original owner and transferring the other portion into a separate account held in the name of the other spouse.

Most employers will immediately distribute the nonemployee spouse's portion of a defined contribution plan (e.g., a 401(k) or savings plan) to that spouse. The nonemployee spouse may choose to either roll this distribution over into an IRA account or take possession of the assets.

If the nonemployee spouse takes possession of the assets, income taxes apply but not excise tax penalties. A distribution from the account at divorce is one of the few instances where retirement assets can be prematurely distributed from a qualified plan without having to pay the penalty.

If the original owner withdraws money from the plan during the divorce or just before the separation, the settlement agreement should specify that this party is responsible for tax consequences associated with the withdrawal. If the parties agree to file a joint tax return as part of the divorce settlement, address the responsibility for income taxes associated with that withdrawal.

Transfer of an individual retirement account (IRA) or individual retirement annuity during the divorce is not a taxable transfer. A QDRO is not necessary to divide or transfer interest in an IRA.

Overpayment of Taxes

A clever way to hide assets is prepayment of taxes. For example, a divorcing couple might be owed a large income tax refund and one spouse might apply it to next year's tax liability. Make certain your spouse has not significantly altered his or her income tax withholding.

Account statements for payments made in the current or prior tax years can be obtained easily from your local IRS office if the payments are made in the names of both spouses. If payments are made separately, your spouse must sign an IRS form authorizing you to have this information.

The other spouse might also prepay property taxes on a home and then negotiate for possession of that home.

Taxing Closely Held Businesses

Be sure to address the tax liabilities associated with a business and also sources of income a party may receive from a closely held business. The IRS may allow a business to take deductions that are appropriate for tax purposes. But the divorce court may consider these deductions as income to a particular spouse for purposes of calculating child support or valuing the company. They include retirement plan contributions, company cars, insurance benefits, travel benefits, travel reimbursements and personal expenditures made by the company on behalf of you or your spouse.

Consult with an accountant and other necessary professionals on the various problems associated with a closely held business. Since the IRS may request an audit at some point, make certain your settlement agreement includes as much protective language as possible.

CHAPTER 24

IF YOU GO TO COURT

EVEN THOUGH most divorce cases settle, one feature unique to Texas law makes going to court a real worry for most people: Texans can request a jury to hear certain family law issues. This fact adds to the circus atmosphere of what is largely an administrative procedure in many other states.

The Family Court Setup in Texas

Divorces in Texas are typically heard through a system of state district courts presided over by judges elected by the people of that jurisdiction.

In the large cities, certain district courts are designated to handle only domestic relations cases, including divorces and child custody matters. The judges of these courts are often experienced family law attorneys who deal exclusively with family issues. Harris County (Houston), for instance, has nine family district courts. Dallas County (Dallas) has seven such courts, while Tarrant County (Fort Worth) has six. In these counties, each family district court also has an associate judge who is assigned to determine temporary and other matters.

In Bexar County (San Antonio), Collin County (Plano and McKinney) and Travis County (Austin), divorce cases are heard in civil district courts that handle other civil cases as well as family law. The counties of Galveston, Harrison (Longview), Midland and El Paso each have one court specifically designated to handle only family law.

District judges in the other Texas counties hear a variety of civil matters, from business lawsuits to divorce.

Because of these varying court setups across the state, court procedures and the quality of justice can be different in Marfa in far West Texas from what they are in Houston. That's not to say that you can't get a fair trial in a small town. But it helps to know something about the judges and the workings of the courts in the jurisdiction where your case is heard. Even if you import a big-city family law specialist to handle your divorce in a rural county, it is usually helpful to have local counsel who can advise you in dealing with a particular judge.

Your First Court Setting

No matter where your divorce is filed, eventually it will be set for trial on the court's calendar if you are unable to reach agreement. Even though as many as 90% of all family law cases settle, one-half of all legal cases filed in the courts of Texas involve some facet of family law. The first court setting usually is three months or more after the filing of the divorce petition. A case is often reset more than once before it actually reaches trial, although in some courts a case could go to trial on a first setting.

Continuances occur for a variety of reasons: the parties may not be ready to try the case, the attorneys or their client may have conflicting schedules, or the court's docket is full. If the judge is already in trial on another case or has an immediate issue to address or an older case to hear, your case may be passed over and continued to a later date.

The parties sometimes jockey for a place on the docket for financial reasons. One spouse will often have to sell assets or transfer them to the other spouse to finalize the divorce. The spouse who will have to pay out money may want the case continued for as long as possible to put off such a move. In some cases, the receiving spouse becomes anxious to settle — even to the point of accepting an inadequate offer — because the other side successfully delays the trial and keeps the assets in limbo. A spouse may also want to slow down the divorce if the other spouse is to receive significant compensation in the near future. Factor in the expenses associated with delay to see if settling now is better than waiting for a potentially greater payday.

Some divorce cases simply must be adjudicated in court. Those cases usually involve revenge, a matter of principle or simply being unable to agree. That's especially true when one spouse believes the other doesn't have the intestinal fortitude to risk the courtroom. Let your spouse know that you will stand up for yourself before, during and after the divorce.

Appearing in Court

You become part of the court system from the moment you get up the morning you are to go to court, and you must take the day seriously. That includes dressing with a respect for the system. For men, a suit or sport coat with slacks, a white or pastel shirt. A tie is optional. Women should be in similar conservative attire. If you're not sure about your wardrobe choices, consult your attorney. Image is important when you are speaking to a judge or jury. In a marital dispute involving finances, your credibility is on the line from the start. It's a subtle thing, but you want to appear worthy of a successful outcome.

Remember to ask your attorney where you should meet in the courthouse. Judges are assigned their own courtroom and the most likely place to meet is in the hallway outside that courtroom. To reach most courtrooms these days, you have to pass through a metal detector. Make sure you do not carry anything that could be considered a weapon and set off the alarm, including mace key chains.

When you appear in court, always act in a mature and professional manner. Because of the emotional nature of many family court actions, there have been threats as well as actual violence perpetrated by one party against another. Judges see this type of behavior and clamp down with a zero tolerance policy.

Always approach your day in court with a calm, cool exterior, although inside your stomach is turning flips. Many cases settle because one party appears so confident in court that he or she scares the other side into settlement. As in most things in life, the party that keeps his or her emotions in check usually wins the day.

Courtroom Cast of Characters

Here are the titles and functions of the people you will encounter in the courtroom:

Judge — In Texas, the judge in family court or a civil district court is an elected official who runs the courtroom. He or she can be the finder of fact or assist the jury in coming to a decision.

Associate Judge — Helps the judge by presiding over temporary hearings and taking the place of the judge on some occasions. This is an appointed position.

Bailiff — This is a uniformed officer of the court who keeps order and enforces the wishes of the judge or master. If one party gets belligerent and the judge holds him or her in contempt, the bailiff takes that person to jail. In jury trials, the bailiff becomes the jury's best friend.

Court Clerk — This person manages the court, including handling all the paperwork necessary to a hearing or trial, posting the court's docket and dealing with the demands of litigants and attorneys.

Court Reporter — This is a job that is changing with advances in technology. Court reporters have been mostly women who take down everything said in court and prepare transcripts for later trials and appeals. Plans are being made in some jurisdictions to computerize this function in the near future.

A Trial Docket Primer

Here is the scene in a modern Texas family court to begin the morning session: the litigants and their witnesses for several cases on the judge's docket fill the courtroom. Outside on hard wooden benches in the hallways, more parties, witnesses and lawyers attempt to resolve their cases before court comes to order.

The judge calls the docket and checks the status of each case with attorneys representing the parties. Those attorneys may want an opportunity to talk settlement, request a continuance or ask to speak with the judge in chambers about a particular issue that needs clarification.

The judge examines those cases that are ready for trial. The oldest case usually has priority. If there is an emergency issue on the docket, the court probably addresses that problem first.

If the judge is in the midst of a trial, he or she will usually proceed with that case and reschedule the others. This is how the judicial system works, and your attorney is powerless to change it. You may prepare for trial and bring your witnesses from all over only to have your case continued.

The best you can expect, in most cases, is for your lawyer to call the courthouse on the day before your case is set to determine where you are on the docket and what cases are set before yours. Some court clerks will tell your lawyer that a trial is in progress or a more pressing case must be resolved before yours can move forward. Other judges may require you, your witnesses and your lawyer to be in court every time the case is set.

Judge or Jury Best in Property Cases?

The Texas Constitution provides that the right to a trial by jury is inviolate, so either party to a divorce or other family matter may request a jury. If such a request is not made, a judge determines the matters at issue.

In any family law case, jury findings regarding the characterization and valuation of property are binding on the court. Decisions on how property is divided are advisory only and may be disregarded by the court. Some cases are better tried to a jury, while others are best before the court. Situations where it may possibly be advantageous to try a family law case to the court include when:

- The case is strong on the facts, as juror emotions may weaken strong facts.
- Some of the evidence may not be admitted, as a judge is more likely to consider such evidence if there is no jury.
- There are time or monetary limitations, as it takes longer for a case to come up for jury trial than for a bench trial, and it takes longer to prepare for a jury trial and to try a case before a jury.
- The judge who presides over the trial has ruled in your favor at hearings for temporary relief or other preliminary matters.

Situations where you might be better off with a jury include when:

- Your case is strong on the law, as jurors tend to see the law in absolutes, while a judge may find limitations.
- You are the petitioner, since you present evidence first and are in the best position to make a good first impression on the jury.
- You want to preserve a strong case for appeal, since there is more chance for error in a case tried to a jury.
- The judge who will hear your case has a history of rulings adverse to litigants in your position or antipathy to your attorney.

Keep Composed on the Stand

The instructions we give people on their first time in court are fairly simple. Focus on the issue at hand. Sit up straight in your seat, speak clearly and be polite. Remember that the finder of fact (judge or jury) is evaluating your responses and your overall demeanor. While on the witness stand, do not become argumentative or hostile with the other lawyer or answer questions in a haughty or sarcastic fashion.

Think of the opposing counsel as a master interrogator. Do not try to be clever. If you feel that he or she is attacking you, do not strike back. The other side may be trying to get you upset and alter your focus. Do not help them achieve their goal.

When the other side questions you, give truthful and accurate answers. Lying on the stand is both unethical and illegal, and more to the point it is impractical. If you are caught lying on the stand, even about some insignificant fact, it may ruin your credibility with the trial judge.

Offering more information than the other lawyer requests can prove the other side's case. Once you answer the question as briefly as possible, don't say another word. If you are concerned about how to answer certain questions, discuss this with your lawyer.

Your lawyer should detail a specific plan for handling the case at trial, based on the information available and how he knows the judge in that court may respond. You may think a fact or piece of evidence is absolutely essential, but it could annoy the judge and throw your lawyer off stride. Most divorce lawyers want to know how you will testify. Your refusal to follow your lawyer's advice may cause you to lose your case.

Basic Rules for Giving Testimony

Always tell the truth.

Listen to the question.

Make certain you understand the question asked.

Be sure to answer the question.

Take your time.

Answer only the question asked.

Answer orally and distinctly.

Do not guess.

Avoid boxing yourself in.

Don't argue with the opposing counsel.

If you forget the question, ask the attorney to repeat it.

Dress appropriately.

It is okay for witnesses or your attorney to have spoken to you.

Do not respond to the question until the opposing attorney completes the question and is silent.

CHAPTER 25

A Divorce Is Granted

IF THE DIVORCE has been agreed to and the parties sign a final decree, only one side and his or her attorney are required to appear in court to prove up the divorce, although attending the final hearing might be psychologically good for you.

"I encourage people to attend the final hearing in their divorce," says family therapist Maryanne Watson. "There should be a ritual to divorce like there is when you marry. I encourage people to go because it is important to have closure. I also talk about the grief that follows, not just the day of the divorce, but later on, when you deal with the many details of the divorce."

The Final Decree

When your divorce is final, the judge signs a document called the final decree of divorce. This document divorces the parties and spells out the terms of the divorce. If the dissolution takes place through a settlement by the parties, the final decree of divorce usually contains a settlement agreement signed by the parties and the judge that makes it binding on both sides. If the case is resolved in trial, the decree spells out the court's ruling or the jury verdict.

As part of the divorce process, your attorney should review the decree and any settlement agreement with you before the divorce is final. Since you can be held in contempt for violations of these terms and conditions, make certain you understand exactly what is required of you.

Emotions are normally at a high level during a trial or settlement talks, so people may forget certain issues such as the exact distribution of proceeds from the sale of the marital residence or who gets which music CDs. Put your copy of the divorce papers in a handy place, since you may need to refer to them in the future as disputes or questions arise.

Details, Details, Details...

Once your divorce is final, either by agreement or in a trial before a judge or jury, you have items to follow up on and tasks to complete. These include the following:

- If you plan to appeal, there are strict time limits, so discuss these with your attorney immediately.
- Change your will, medical directive and power of attorney.
- Prepare and file real estate deeds transferring property interests.
- Transfer titles or bills of sale to automobiles, boats or other property.
- Enter a Qualified Domestic Relations Order (QDRO)

to divide a retirement account.

- Prepare and file insurance forms with change of beneficiary.
- Make sure you have health insurance in force.
- For women, request a name change with the correct governmental entity and creditors. (NOTE: The name change should be ordered in the final decree.)
- Inform creditors and others of address change as well as name change.
- Change name and address on bank accounts.
- File IRS Form 8332 to establish dependency exemptions.
- If applicable, file Income Withholding Orders for child support collection.

Still Upset? Try an Appeal

You might expect half of all divorcing people to feel they were treated badly in the divorce process. But one study of attitudes following divorce indicates that as many as 80% of litigants feel they were taken to the cleaners in the process. That's an overwhelming percentage, and it tells an interesting story about those who enter the divorce process. Apparently, both sides in a divorce often come away with a bad taste in their mouths.

If you feel cheated, you may file a motion to set aside the decree or request a new trial. Under Texas law, the motion generally must be filed within 30 days of the court order. However, other post-judgment actions may need to occur sooner.

Koons Fuller partner (and co-author) Heather King handles a number of family law appeals. She realizes how difficult they are and how important it is to move quickly through the process.

Most of the appeals she has handled are those she did not try initially, although she sometimes handles a case from beginning to end. In her experience, it's always better to have more than one set of eyes looking at the case. You should consult with a family law appeals lawyer as soon as possible after you obtain an unfavorable judgment to review your options and possibly avoid the necessity of an appeal.

A motion for a new trial is rarely successful unless the court failed to consider a material fact in evidence or the court made an error in its ruling. Remember that the judge considering this motion is the same one who heard your entire case. A motion for a new trial is asking the judge to admit that he or she made a mistake serious enough to warrant correction. The judge is not likely to admit such a mistake without clear and convincing evidence.

If your motion fails, consider an appeal to a higher court. Either party to a divorce has the right to appeal the final decree, although most appeals fail. In divorce cases, most successful appeals deal with such issues as the trial judge not allowing a key witness to testify or another major error on the part of the trial judge, usually involving a mistake of law.

If you reach this point, you and your attorney should evaluate your chances of a successful appeal versus the tremendous cost in time and money.

From the trial court, appeals proceed to the Texas Court of Appeals. There are 14 such courts located in various cities across the state. Each Court of Appeals has up to 13 sitting judges. A three-judge panel from one of these courts hears your appeal. If you are not satisfied with the actions of the appellate court, you can apply to the Texas Supreme Court to review your case. But unlike the Court of Appeals, the Supreme Court does not automatically accept a case for appeal. The state's highest court decides which cases it will hear. Appealing a divorce case all the way to the Texas Supreme Court is rare and expensive and can be very complicated.

With each appeal, you have to pay for a copy of the court file (clerk's record) and a copy of the trial transcript (reporter's record), in addition to paying your lawyer to write a history of the case. If you hire a different lawyer to handle your appeal, that lawyer has to spend many hours becoming familiar with the facts of the case before writing the appeal brief. If the appeal is not successful with the Court of Appeals, the lawyer may have to draft other documents and briefs for the Supreme Court, and that means additional expense.

Seeking redress through the appeals process is possible, but it's much more difficult than handling the case properly at trial.

HE SAID
SHE SAID: A National Hot-Button Issue

<u>He said</u> the divorce devastated him. When their relationship was over, he hated not being able to see his son every day. She didn't understand how much he enjoyed roughhousing on the lawn or reading bedtime stories.

Since they signed the divorce decree, she complained about everything. He couldn't be a day late on his child support payments or a minute late after a weekend visit. She criticized the way their son looked following those weekends. Before they divorced, she told everyone what a good, active father he was. Now he was suddenly the world's worst.

To heck with her, he thought. He looked forward to his son's weekend visits, carefully planning their activities and making sure the fridge was stocked with his favorite food. Those weekends were always great. It gave them a chance to reconnect and bond.

When he told her that he would like to see his son more during the week, she pulled out the divorce papers and told him he should have thought of that before he signed. He regretted not asking for more time, but he really thought she would be more flexible.

Then she started seeing someone new. The relationship moved fast and within six months, they married. Her new husband was okay, but another man was spending more time with his son than he was. Those weekend visits seemed even more important. He didn't want this new man taking his only son away.

So he met with his lawyer about going to court to get the child custody agreement modified. He wanted more visitation and felt he had a good case. His son told him over and over that he wanted to spend more time with him. He was a good father who gave her extra money when she asked him to pay for swim lessons.

Before he could file papers for the modification, she served him papers. He could not believe what he was reading. She notified him that in 60 days, she and his son were moving 1,500 miles away. In the divorce decree, she had the right to designate the primary residence without regard to geographic location. Her new husband took a better job offer on the East Coast and they would join him there.

He was outraged. He immediately contacted his attorney and let her know that he was going to fight the move. She had to suspect he wouldn't give in that easily.

<u>She said</u> the divorce was hard on everyone. She tried to move past the anger and hurt feelings, for the sake of their son, but all the little things she hated about him when they were married seemed amplified now that they were divorced.

She hated the way he always gave their son exactly what he wanted. When he went to visit his father, he had no rules, ate junk food and never went to bed at a decent time. That meant for a week after one of his "father-son" weekends, her son was a brat and had to be retrained on the rules of her house. The transition was never smooth.

He was that way when they were married, and she was always the heavy. Now she didn't control anything. He was always late returning their son on Sunday evenings. When she asked him to make sure the boy bathed over the weekend, he would shrug his shoulders and say, "He's a boy. He's going to get dirty, play hard and hate baths. Who am I to take that away from him?" He didn't have a clue what it was like to be a real parent and enforce rules on their son.

She also felt he was instigating war with her, begging for more visitation. No way was she going to relent. It was stressful for their son to visit every other weekend. Increasing the overnight visits with him would ruin their son's routine.

She didn't expect to meet someone and fall in love as quickly as they did. But her new husband was wonderful. He got along with her son and was a good role model.

Shortly after she remarried, he began to pester her for more visitation. She could tell he was uncomfortable with another man spending so much time with their son. She asked him to give her new husband a chance, explaining that he was a really good man. Instead of being reassured, he became even more insecure.

When her new husband got the job offer that would double his salary, they made the difficult decision to relocate. It wasn't an easy decision, but with the increase in his salary they could afford private school for the boy and she could spend more time with him. She knew her ex would not be happy. But they had valid reasons for the move that would benefit their son. And since the "domicile" of her son was not restricted in the divorce decree, they were going.

With the decision made, she instructed her attorney to draft the notice letter. She hoped they could find a way to compromise.

The result was a court battle that was costlier and more contentious than their divorce. He felt the move would rob him of his son. He asked for more visitation time when she was doing the exact opposite.

She could see nothing but the positive attributes of this move. The higher income would greatly benefit her son by providing him with a more comfortable and privileged life. She agreed to let their son stay with him over much of the summer and share school breaks.

In the end, they relocated. In addition to allowing him increased visitation during the summer, she was ordered to pay the cost of all transportation for their son's trips to and from Texas.

CHAPTER 26

RELOCATING A CHILD AND OTHER MODIFICATIONS

THE FINAL DECREE of divorce is a living, breathing document, especially if the couple has children or if payments must be made from one ex to the other in the future.

Both parties often spend months after the divorce determining how flexible to be with its provisions as lives change and children get older. Only the two parents can decide if everything in the decree is to be taken literally or if the document is simply a guideline.

Changes happen in every family. Must you panic at every proposed change, or are you ready to go with the flow? When these changes come up, each side must ask themselves the following questions:

- Will this change cost me money and create a hardship?
- Is this change better for the children and for myself?
- Will the change be short or long term?
- Although I may be okay with this change, will it lay the groundwork for a change down the road that I don't want?

• Do we both understand the limitations of this change?
• Must we put this change in writing, or should we keep it verbal?
• Can I trust my ex to do this unofficially, or should I have my attorney "paper" it?

Major life changes, known in family law as material and substantial changes of circumstance, are often subjects of efforts to legally modify a divorce decree as it relates to the children. The most common modifications involve child custody, support and visitation. Many modification agreements are made without court approval. But if one parent later reneges on the agreement, it may not be enforceable. If there is any residual friction between parents, it's best to obtain a court order.

Relocating a Child

Lately, the most contentious type of modification has been the attempt to relocate children from one city or state to another. Relocation is often a contested issue in a divorce, but it arises more commonly in modification actions when one parent seeks to move the children away from the area where the other parent lives. The shift toward joint custody has led to an increased occurrence of residence restrictions. Many states, including Texas, are struggling with the relocation issue.

At odds are two legal rights. On the one hand, any person in this country has a constitutional right to mobility. We allow people to move freely from one place to another with no restrictions. The Texas Family Code even provides that one of the parents be in charge of determining where the children will reside on a primary basis. On the other hand, that very same code says children have the right to frequent and continuing access by both parents, and that it's in their best interest.

A problem arises when the parent designated the sole managing conservator, or the parent with primary possession of the children, attempts to relocate them far enough away from the other parent to make visitation and a continuing relationship between the children and the other parent more difficult. Does the moving parent have the right to take the children or is it in the best interest of the children for them to stay near the non-moving parent? These relocations not only cause emotional upheavals, but they can create financial difficulties, too. Here are two examples:

> **The divorced mother of three children meets a man and falls in love. He is the heir to a family fortune and runs his family's business in another state. The children's father pays some child support and spends a great deal of time with his kids. The boyfriend asks the woman to marry him and move to his city with her children. What right is most important here?**

> **A man with sole custody of his young daughter gets an ultimatum from his employer: accept a transfer to another city or find another job. The girl's mother is a recovering drug addict who is getting into shape to spend time with her daughter. What should the father do?**

Attitudes toward residence restrictions vary greatly among the courts, practicing attorneys and social scientists. Dr. Judith

Wallerstein, writing in the *Family Law Quarterly* (with Tony J. Tanke), argues that support for the primary custodial parent-child relationship should supersede joint parental access because the well-being of the primary custodial parent and the child are inexorably linked, but the child's well-being and the noncustodial parent's visitation are not. This attitude is receiving increased support from the higher courts in Texas.

Dallas social scientist Dr. Jan DeLipsey represents the other side of this argument. She believes that having two parents in close proximity is better for children regardless of other factors. She states that meaningful parenting means parenting under all conditions and circumstances: health, sickness, successes and failures, and that a good parent is available to a child. Dr. DeLipsey asserts that moving a child from his or her other parent stresses and often disrupts psychologically important parent-child relationships, which may have adverse consequences. This is a popular approach taken by many courts across the country to encourage contact between a child and both parents.

The Texas Family Code does not directly address this subject. But in *Lenz v. Lenz*, the Texas Supreme Court allowed the mother to relocate her children back to her home in Germany. The high court will certainly have more to say on this issue in the future.

Change of Custody

Relocation is an example of a change in circumstances that could become the reason to ask for a change in custody of the children. A full-blown custody trial is the most extreme example of an attempted modification. The parent asking for a change in custody or possession of a child must show that the modification would be in the best interest of the child. He or she must also show that the circumstances of the child or one of the parents has materially and substantially changed since the current agreement was made or a court order issued. You should think long and hard about the effect of any return to the court system. Is this action necessary for the child, or are you just upset? Are there other ways to accomplish what you want? And will the positive effect of the modification offset the negative effect of bringing the action?

Just consider the expense. "Going for custody" can be one of the most expensive court moves you can make. The money you spend in attorney's fees, expert witnesses and probably lost income during that time might purchase a very nice education for your children.

More or Less Child Support

If the income of either spouse increases or decreases significantly, the amount of child support may be adjusted. Look at the overall financial situation before going to court and forcing your ex to pay more support. If he or she spends money on the children above and beyond child support, could those expenditures be endangered if you play hardball in the courts?

Talk to your lawyer, who can assist you in calculating the projected new child support payments under your facts. You can determine if those extra payments equal or exceed the amount you would get if you took the matter back to court.

Sometimes parents obligated to pay child support take defensive actions when called upon to pay more. Increasing child support is another reason some parents seek custody of their children. Actions like this often fail, but they create additional expense for the custodial parent who is seeking an increase in child support.

The fear of a custody battle is amplified if a parent has less than exemplary conduct since the divorce. Living with a friend of the opposite sex may not cause you to lose your children, but it can muddy the waters.

Modifying Visitation

Children get older and circumstances change. A noncustodial parent may want more visitation, or the child may become a teenager and want to spend more time with his or her friends instead of going to a parent's house. A child may want to spend an entire summer backpacking with an uncle across Europe.

Modifications are expensive if you have to go to court. You might spend several thousands of dollars for an extra evening of visitation or to deny your ex that amount of time with the children.

"Working through a divorce, there is an actual process of grieving and working through that sense of loss. No matter how bad the relationship is, it's the end of a dream. The dream was of a family being together and they have to grieve the death of the dream and work through the grief process before they can move on."

Dr. Maryanne Watson

CHAPTER 27

GETTING ON WITH YOUR LIFE

THE MOTION PICTURE *Sideways* dealt with a character who engages in the practice of "drink and dial," calling his ex-wife well into an evening of fine wines. How many of us have known divorced people who simply couldn't let go of a lost love? It's a natural human quality, but is it healthy?

It has been said that people don't go to divorce court for justice. At the most, what they can expect is a conclusion. The very nature of divorce may make it impossible to bring fairness into an emotionally destructive process so that everyone is happy. People may spend years being angry with a former spouse and bitter over facts that cannot be changed. While a certain amount of emotion and anger is justified, don't ruin the rest of your life worrying about the behavior of others. When one door closes, a window opens. We recommend that people look for a window to open rather than spending time banging their heads against a closed door. Some therapists and counselors actually practice something called marriage disengagement therapy, helping people move out of a marriage so they can go forward into the future.

"Plenty of people have a hard time letting go so they can move on," says Dr. Maryanne Watson. "I see people needing this quite frequently, and it's typically the one who didn't want the divorce. When people hold on to these feelings, they often have a host of physical problems. High blood pressure, migraines, depression. Not to mention, it's not much fun to be around a person who is oozing anger. If you become a negative person, people are not going to want to be around you. It's in your best interest to not hang on to these sorts of things."

You have to look at the big picture and see your life over the long haul. Sure, your children will be upset when you tell them about the divorce, and for a time after. But studies show that after the first six months, kids generally rebound and do even better than they were prior to the divorce, when tensions in the home were often strained.

When Confronted, Choose Reason

We find that the happiest people after a divorce are those who feel generous enough to be fair with the person who once inspired them to hate and dread. The idea that you must never back down, allow no compromise and stick to your guns does nothing for you in the family court system and very little in life.

If you can afford to be generous with your ex (and especially your children), do it. Here's an example of that:

A man with two children agreed to pay $1,200 a month in child support after the divorce. As time went

**along, he also picked up the cost of music lessons and
tuition to a music camp for his kids, and worked with
his ex to establish college funds for both children. He
was not obligated to do all this, except for the obligation
any good parent would feel.**

**When the man asked to extend his weekend visita-
tion so he could take the children with him and his new
wife to their lake cabin on Sunday, at first the children's
mother refused. She still felt he had disappointed her,
but the sincerity of his commitment to the children was
so strong that she couldn't deny him. He was reasonable
and responsible, and she came to the conclusion that she
had no choice but to relent.**

Reason and generosity often trump toughness at this point.
Your children will respect you for your restraint and it may even
make your ex easier to deal with over the long haul.

But When Reason Doesn't Work...

When one party to a divorce simply won't play by the rules,
an enforcement action for contempt may be necessary. These
actions are used to enforce the payment of child support and
attorney's fees, compel child custody or visitation orders and
control certain types of financial and property matters.

Contempt of court is one of the remedies of an enforcement
action. The standard for contempt is fairly understandable. One
party must willfully refuse to comply with a specific order of the
court that is central to the obligation in question. For example,
if a payor spouse fails to send child support or maintenance

payments, even though he or she has worked and instead has chosen to spend the money on other things, most likely this is contempt.

A contempt action involves the court putting the opposing party in jail, assessing a fine or both for failure to comply with the divorce decree. Sometimes an action like this is necessary to convince the offending party that this is serious business.

Under a contempt action, you or your ex may be placed in jail and can only be released by purging the conduct in question. For example, the court may order you to jail until all or most of the back payments are made. If you are truly unable to pay, the court may not keep you in jail. But you'd be surprised how often relatives or close friends come forward with the cash to pay the amount due.

For many people, these support payments are essential to the maintenance of an ongoing household. Don't let the paying spouse slide or something that seems to be a one-time occurrence can become a regular problem. Sometimes people make threats to withhold support payments, and those threats should be taken seriously. If the party begins to act contemptuously toward you, keep detailed records of obligations that are not met.

Once your ex misses a payment or two, don't wait too long to file a contempt action. Some of the most patient people wait until they are owed tens of thousands of dollars before making a move. In cases like this, you may have to accept installment payments to enable the opposing party to pay off the large debt.

Your relationship with the offending party is directly related to your initial actions after the divorce. If you file a contempt action immediately after the party fails to comply, this will send a signal that you will punish noncompliance. You need to establish that you will not tolerate missed support payments and that the other party must comply with the financial arrangements either agreed to or ordered by the court.

You will be accused of being inflexible, but just remind your ex that those you owe money to are even less flexible. By being steadfast, you may be able to modify future behavior.

CHAPTER 28

PRENUPS AND POSTNUPS: ANTICIPATING ANOTHER MARRIAGE

PEOPLE WITH LARGE ASSETS are often wary about marriage, fearing that a potential spouse might be more interested in a large property settlement than a long and loving marital relationship. One way to make that big financial decision and still feel protected is to execute a premarital agreement, or "prenup."

Historically, extremely well-to-do people use prenups to protect themselves from gold diggers and charlatans. As the available pool of wealthy people increases over time, prenups gain favor with a wider group of people whose minds are eased by the protective aspects of these agreements.

A prenup is simply a premarital financial contract that may confirm or modify the characterization of property. The contract must be agreed to and signed by both parties. It is common for premarital agreements to confirm that certain assets brought into the marriage by one party remain that party's separate property.

The property addressed in the prenup may be an interest in real or personal property, retirement benefits, stock options and leasehold interests. A prenup may also provide that a spouse's income and earnings are that spouse's separate property.

People of middle-class means increasingly use prenups. A person with a job and few liquid assets might execute a premarital agreement to protect his or her retirement account or future earnings in case of divorce, separation or death.

Prenups tend to simplify financial situations that become complicated and messy at the point of divorce. For instance, some assets are not easily divisible, such as an interest in a family-owned business or a large tract of real estate. If one spouse owns a portion of that hard-to-divide property as his or her separate property, a premarital agreement could keep the entire asset from being divided or sold.

"One situation where prenups make sense is when you have one person with significant assets and one with very little," says Dodee Crockett. "If you have significant wealth and children, and your fiancee has children and very few accumulated assets, you may not want to wind up leaving your hard-earned money to your new stepchildren."

Crockett says that if the person you are marrying is honorable, a prenup should not bother that person. "If you are made to feel guilty because you want the agreement," she says, "then maybe it's worth a little more courtship."

Prenups are never just financial instruments, but you should look at them in the same light as you would any contract, Crockett says. "When both people have significant assets, you are talking about something more like a corporate merger than simply the marriage of two people. You wouldn't take on a business partner without checking into their background and spelling out ownership of the assets."

What's Protected By a Prenuptial Agreement?

The following matters may be addressed in a prenup:

- The rights and obligations to property by either party
- The right to buy, sell, use, transfer, exchange, abandon, lease, consume, assign, create a security interest in, mortgage, encumber, dispose of or otherwise manage and control property
- The disposition of property on separation, marital dissolution or death
- The modification or elimination of spousal support
- The making of a will, trust or other arrangement to carry out the provisions of the agreement
- Ownership of a life insurance policy
- Choice of law governing the agreement
- Any personal matter not in violation of public policy or criminal statutes
- Waiving of homestead rights
- Providing income from all separate property to remain separate property, precluding creation of any community property during marriage and partitioning future earnings

A prenuptial agreement cannot be written to adversely affect the right of a child to support in the event of divorce. Agreements for private education, college expenses or cars for children, though, might be enforceable as long as they don't violate public policy, even if they infringe on a parent's rights or are against a child's best interest.

Firm partner Aubrey Connatser, who often negotiates prenups, reports the trend of people using these agreements as inducements to marry or to control a future spouse's behavior.

"They're getting signing bonuses," she says. "Two hundred fifty thousand dollars in a separate account to salve the hurt of having to sign a prenup." Connatser says she has heard of people even setting out the amount of sex the couple will have, how quickly they will have children and whether one party has to lose weight or quit smoking.

Why a Postnuptial Agreement?

Postnups are much like prenups in the way they deal with assets, except that they are executed after the marriage. Like premarital agreements, postnups must be in writing and signed by the parties. The agreement also must specify that the parties intend to actually partition and exchange property.

Through the use of a postnup, spouses may convert community property or their separate property into the other spouse's separate property. Sometimes a married person agrees to partition assets into the separate property of the other spouse to protect the property from creditors. In the event of a divorce, the property is already divided.

How to Enforce or Break These Agreements

Prenuptial or postnuptial agreements are tough-to-break financial contracts. Texas law presumes that such agreements are enforceable. The burden of proof, therefore, is on the party attacking the agreement to show that it is not valid.

To contest the validity of an agreement, the party must first show that it was not signed voluntarily or that it is "unconscionable." To determine if a prenup or postnup is unconscionable, the court must look at the entire atmosphere in which the agreement was made; alternatives available to the parties, if any, at the time the agreement was made; the non-bargaining ability of one party; whether the agreement is illegal or against public policy; and whether the contract is oppressive or unreasonable.

If the court declares the agreement unconscionable, the contesting party must then prove that he or she was not provided a fair and reasonable disclosure of the other party's property or finances; did not voluntarily waive disclosure beyond what was provided; and did not have adequate knowledge of the other party's property or finances.

Several Texas cases show how difficult it is to overturn such an agreement. In one case, the appellate court upheld an agreement even when the wife did not have an attorney, did not read or understand the agreement and had no understanding of the effect of the agreement's terms. In another, the Houston Court of Appeals upheld an agreement despite the husband's contention that the parties had disparate bargaining power, he signed the agreement shortly before the wedding, he was not represented by counsel and the agreement was allegedly one-sided.

In a third case, the court held that "the mere fact that a party made a hard bargain does not allow him relief from a freely and voluntarily assumed contract."

The issue of whether a prenup or postnup stands up in court must be evaluated on a case-by-case basis. But because a well-written premarital agreement is difficult to overturn, don't just sign one and figure you will address its validity later.

CHAPTER 29

Never Again

WHEN WE SAY, "Never again," we are not advising you never to fall in love, get married or place your trust in people ever again after a divorce. You are entitled to happiness, whatever happiness means for you.

This is what you should not ever do again: stay ignorant of the financial details of your family, the money foibles of your loved one or how to protect your assets in the event of another divorce.

What you should do is the following:

- Consider some kind of premarital agreement that simply spells out financial rules between you.
- Always be the documented spouse who keeps financial records at your fingertips.
- Thoroughly review income tax forms, contracts and other financial instruments before signing them.
- During the marriage, periodically examine reports from the three major credit bureaus to know how many

accounts you have and how your household income is being used.

- If you are unfortunate enough to face another divorce, learn from your experience.
- You should know how to divide community assets more productively.
- If you are owed some kind of support payments over time, require life insurance on the paying spouse.
- You should know how to best handle disposition of the marital residence, retirement plans and deferred compensation programs such as stock options.
- You should know that in most cases, you cannot depend on receiving alimony in Texas, but child support is ordered in almost every case. The amount of child support is something you can usually calculate.

Never again will you be in the dark about your financial standing, and that's a good thing whether you get a divorce tomorrow or live with the same person the rest of your life.

Appendices

Appendix A — Texas Professionals List

Appendix B — Glossary of Family Law Terms

Appendix C — Texas Family Code Subchapter C. Child
Support Guidelines

Appendix D — Preparing For Your Deposition

Appendix E — Post-Divorce Checklist

Appendix F — IRS Form 8332 Dependent Exemption

Appendix G — Credit Report Request Letter

Appendix A

TEXAS PROFESSIONALS LIST

The following is a list of professionals with experience helping Texas residents through divorce. This list is a resource for
divorcing people attempting to solve problems unique to their
situation. Although the people listed here are experienced at
divorce situations, neither the authors nor the publishers guarantee the services of these providers.

Dallas

Accountants

Martin E. Auerbach, CPA
972-239-4699

Alan H. Levi, CPA
214-559-0008

Vance K. Maultsby, Jr., CPA
214-739-4737

Hunter Nibert
972-661-1843

*Financial Planners
/Wealth Managers*

Todd Amacher
972-858-1100

Eric Bennett
214-252-3250

Dodee Crockett
214-750-2107

Greg Hall
214-252-3266

David Heil
972-943-7255

Christopher Holtby
214-706-9053

Mike Jarvis
972-455-9060

Kevin W. Margolis
972-960-6460, ext. 5

Susan Rouke
214-515-4874

Chris Sheppard
817-420-5064

Nancy Wilcox-Mello
972-384-2036

Vickie Wise
214-346-3940

Estate Planners

W. Thomas Finley
214-740-1431

Larry Flournoy Jr.
214-599-7000

Michael Kaufman
214-953-5734

Alan C. Klein
214-369-3889

Edward V. Smith, III
214-599-7000

Lawrence M. Wolfish
972-248-4656

Counselors

Thom Allen
214-498-8466

Barry S. Coakley, PhD
972-406-1077

Alexandria H. Doyle, PhD
214-361-5900

Gail B. Inman
214-599-0505

Kevin Karlson
972-839-2394

Ray Levy, PhD
972-407-1191

Patrick Savage
214-526-3374

Honey Sheff, PhD
972-733-0075

Jeffrey C. Siegel, PhD
972-960-1472

Linda Solomon
214-361-8771

Maryanne Watson, PhD
972-380-8600

Psychiatrists

Dr. Philip Korenman, MD
972-985-4011

Realtors

Kay Hayden
972-733-9207

Jan Richey
972-733-7144

Kim Salisbury
214-558-7295

Saundra Stephens Woodmansee
214-520-4424

Mortgage Brokers

Joe Anderson
800-669-6020,
ext. 6293

Angela Deaton
214-738-5874

Kendall Richards
214-642-3846

Mike Wolfe
972-588-9450

Business Valuation Experts

Bill Barnard
972-661-1843

Doug Fejer
972-713-9300

David N. Fuller
972-831-7907

Elizabeth Ann Schrupp
214-349-0654

Forensic CPAs

Doug Fejer
972-831-7907

Vance K. Maultsby, Jr.
214-739-4737

Elizabeth Ann Schrupp
214-349-0654

Jim Wingate
214-750-0640

Bankruptcy Attorneys

Michelle Mendez
972-419-1261

Tax Attorneys

Charles Billings
972-387-2513

Private Investigators

Duane Krueger
214-599-9494

*Retirement/Employment
Benefits Attorney*

Bill Clifton
214-891-7014

Real Estate Appraisers

Marquett Brewster
972-608-2948

Jim Goodrich
972-529-2828

Austin

Accountants

Jan Demetri
512-477-7696

Janet Hagy
512-346-3782

Marcia C. Threadgill, CPA
512-794-9596

*Financial Planners
/Wealth Managers*

Jan Demetri
512-477-7696

Beth Dickson
713-599-1220

Vivian Kolenda
512-795-2160

Mary Ann Osborne
512-420-9825

Estate Planners

Patricia T. Barnes
512-328-8355

Kevin Holcomb
512-480-5600

Mark Schreiber
512-477-7543

Counselors

Diane Ireson, LCSW, BCD
512-306-8044

Tina Moody, M.Div.,
M.A., LPC
512-689-4330

Psychologists

Dr. Larry Miller
512-502-1882

Dr. D. Ross Miller
512-346-2332

Realtors

Dana Dean
512-472-3336

Susie Dudley
512-327-4800

Connie McGlothlin
512-554-3387

Mortgage Brokers

Nikki Bryant
512-413-1164

Bob Goodwin
512-241-3192

Business Valuation Experts

John Anderson
512-476-4873

Edward C. Fowler,
CFA, ASA
512-476-8866

Forensic CPAs

John Anderson
512-476-4873

Marcia C. Threadgill, CPA
512-794-9596

Bankruptcy Attorneys

Leslie Howe
512-472-2888

Tax Attorneys

Michael L. Cook
512-499-3849

James Martens
512-542-9898

Private Investigators

Claude Bookout
512-853-9084

*Retirement/Employment
Benefits Attorney*

Susan Burton
512-472-8800

Real Estate Appraisers

Brad Beal
512-477-7059

San Antonio

Accountants

Kimberly C. Ford, CPA
210-340-8351

Gerald L. Hill, CPA
210-340-8351

Billy J. Tiller, CPA, CVA
210-377-3734

Estate Planners

James C. Woo
210-349-6484

Kevin P. Kennedy
210-824-0771

Counselors

Irv Loev, Ph.D.
210-340-0270

Robin B. Walton
210-223-0779

Psychologists

Dr. Joann Murphey
210-495-0221

Dr. Dina Trevino
210-647-7712

Realtors

Tricia Curbello
210-861-1197

*Business Valuation Experts,
Forensic CPAs*

Gerald L. Hill, CPA
210-340-8351

Billy J. Tiller,
CPA, CVA
210-377-3734

Bankruptcy Attorneys

William R. Davis, Jr.
210-736-6600

Tax Attorneys

Kevin P. Kennedy
210-824-0771

Private Investigators

Gary Barnes
210-824-6300

Houston

Accountants

Geoffrey Poll, CPA, JD
713-783-5200

*Financial Planners
/Wealth Managers*

Jeff Swantkowski
713-344-9302

Estate Planners/Estate Lawyers

Bernard (Barney) Jones
713-621-3330

Scott A. Schepps
713-840-7710

Psychiatrists/Psychologists

Karen Gollaher, PsyD
713-776-9449

*Business Valuation Experts
/Forensic CPAs*

Patrice Ferguson
713-783-5200

Haran Levy, CPA, CVA
713-407-3848

Jeannie McClure
713-622-6000

Private Investigators

Robert Grieve
713-963-9916

Real Estate Appraisers

Cary Coole
713-783-5357

Tyler

*Financial Planners
/Wealth Managers*

Ken Dun
903-534-4000

Estate Planners/Estate Lawyers

Michael D. Allen
903-534-0006

John Berry
903-561-4200

Mark Boon
903-759-2200

Counselors

Dr. Gayle Burress, Ph.D., LPC
903-592-5455

Jack Gilbert, MA, LPC
903-759-7881

Dr. Robert Sperry
903-534-5968

Business Valuation Experts

Robert Bailes
903-561-5859

William (Rusty) Bundy
903-597-6311

Tony Morgan
903-534-0088

Marion Shilling
903-561-8122

Bankruptcy Attorneys

William (Bill) Lively, Jr.
903-593-3001

David B. Long
903-593-7797

Michael J. McNally
903-597-6301

Private Investigators

Paul Black
903-596-8840

Rick and Beverly Lambert
903-316-6161

Real Estate Appraisers

Mike Floyd
903-526-6700

Appendix B

GLOSSARY OF FAMILY LAW TERMS

-A-

ACTION: A lawsuit or proceeding in a court of law.

AFFIDAVIT: A written statement under oath.

ALIMONY or MAINTENANCE: Periodic payments of support provided by one spouse to the other.

ANNULMENT: The marriage is declared void, as though it never took place.

ANSWER: The written response to a complaint, petition or motion.

APPEAL: A legal action where the losing party requests that a higher court review the decision.

ASSET: Everything owned by you or your spouse, including property, cars, furniture, bank accounts, jewelry, life insurance policies, businesses and retirement plans.

ASSOCIATE JUDGE: Hears cases like a judge in court. An associate judge's ruling can be appealed to the district judge.

-B-

BENCH TRIAL: A trial where the judge determines all fact issues and there is no jury.

BILLING: An accounting of hours spent on your case by the attorney, his legal assistant and others. Usually calculated monthly.

BUSINESS VALUATION: Experts are used to value businesses in a divorce context. The valuation of a closely held business or professional practice is only as good as the judgment of the appraiser and the accuracy of the information relied upon. When valuing a closely held business, it is essential to have a thorough knowledge of the measures of value, the methods of valuation and Texas case law. The valuation of professional practices requires a clear understanding of professional goodwill, and there may be a need for adjustments to the value of a business due to its lack of marketability, the size of the interest (minority or majority) and the existence or non-existence of a covenant not to compete.

-C-

CHARACTERIZATION: The process of identifying what property is separate property and what property is community property. The court can only divide the parties' community property and not their separate property.

CHILD SUPPORT: Money paid from one parent to the other for the benefit of their minor children.

CLOSELY HELD BUSINESS: A business that is privately owned, such as a family business.

CLOSING ARGUMENTS: Final statements by each attorney at the end of the trial when they argue to the judge or jury the evidence and the law.

COMMINGLING ASSETS: When separate and community funds are commingled in a manner such that they cannot be identified, it is presumed that the entire fund consists of community property.

COMMON LAW MARRIAGE: A common law marriage comes about when a man and woman who are free to marry agree to live together as husband and wife without a formal ceremony. To be married under common law in Texas, both spouses must agree to be husband and wife, they must live together in Texas as husband and wife and they must hold themselves out to the public as husband and wife.

COMMUNITY DEBTS: Debts undertaken during the marriage are presumed to be community debts; this presumption, however, can be rebutted by a showing that the creditor agreed to look to the separate estate of the spouse incurring the debt for satisfaction of the debt and separate funds were actually used to repay the debt.

COMMUNITY PROPERTY: Property, other than separate property, acquired by either spouse during their marriage. All property that either spouse owns or possesses at divorce is presumed to be community property. This presumption can be rebutted by clear and convincing evidence of a spouse claiming that disputed property is his or her separate property.

CONTEMPT: Failure to follow a court order. One side can request that the court determine that the other side is in contempt for violating a court order and punish him or her.

CONTESTED ISSUES: Any or all issues upon which the parties are unable to agree and which must be resolved by the judge or jury at a hearing or trial.

CONTINGENT ASSET: An asset that you may receive or get later, such as a recovery from a lawsuit or a potential cause of action against a third party.

CONTINGENT LIABILITY: A liability that you may owe later, such as payments for lawsuits against either party or a guaranty that you have signed.

CONTINUANCE: Postponement of a trial or hearing.

CORROBORATING WITNESS: A person who testifies for you and backs up your story.

COUNTERPETITION: A written request to the court for legal action, which is filed by a respondent after being served with a divorce petition.

COURT REPORTER: The person who records the testimony and court proceedings.

CUSTODY (SOLE AND JOINT): Refers to the rights and duties that parents have with respect to their children. Texas uses the terms "sole managing conservator" and "joint managing conservator."

-D-

DECREE: The final document that the judge signs granting the divorce. The divorce decree contains all of the agreements of the parties and orders of the court with respect to all issues in the case, including custody, possession, child support, alimony and a division of the marital estate.

DEFAULT: A party's failure to answer a motion or petition after having been properly served.

DEFERRED COMPENSATION: Deferred compensation includes pensions, annuities payable in the future and other forms of deferred income.

DEPOSITION: Discovery in which an attorney asks questions of the opposing party under oath.

DIRECT EXAMINATION: Questions asked of witnesses called by the attorney asking the questions.

DISCOVERY: A way of getting information from the other side or other people. Examples are interrogatories (written questions to be answered under oath), requests to produce documents and depositions.

DISSOLUTION: The legal end of a marriage.

DOCKET: A court's calendar of cases.

-E-

ENJOINED: Prohibited by the court from doing or failing to do a specific act.

EX PARTE: Communication with the judge by only one party. In order for a judge to speak with either party, the other party must have been properly notified and have an opportunity to be heard.

EXPERT WITNESS: An expert who is qualified in a certain area may testify as to his or her opinion as to the matters in which he or she is qualified. When the spouses' testimony as to the value of certain assets is widely disparate, the court may be more likely to accept a valuation supported by expert opinion. Experts in a family law case may include psychologists, business valuation experts, real estate appraisers, forensic CPA's, and others, such as art and airplane appraisers.

-F -

FILING: Giving the court clerk your legal papers to be included in the court's file.

FORENSIC ACCOUNTANT: A person who prepares an investigation of finances or traces assets for the purpose of discovering information in a lawsuit and offering testimony in court.

-G-

GOODWILL: There are two types of goodwill: Business goodwill (also called commercial goodwill) is the business's reputation and ability, as an institution, to attract and hold business even with a change in ownership. Personal goodwill is associated with the individual professional, not the practice or business as a whole, and therefore cannot be transferred to a buyer. Personal goodwill (also called professional goodwill) does not possess value or constitute an asset separate and apart from the person of the professional, or from the professional's ability to practice the profession. Personal goodwill is not divisible on divorce and is not to be considered in the valuation of the professional's practice.

-H-

HEARING: A legal proceeding before a judge or associate judge on a motion.

I-

INFORMAL DISCOVERY: The voluntary and informal exchange of information between the parties through their attorneys, as distinguished from formal discovery (i.e., interrogatories and requests to produce documents.

INJUNCTION: An order from a court prohibiting a person from doing something.

INTERROGATORIES: Written questions submitted to a party in a divorce for that party to answer under oath.

INVENTORY AND APPRAISEMENT: The first step in identifying a couple's assets and liabilities. Typically both spouses will complete and sign under oath an Inventory and Appraisement setting forth all real and personal property owned or claimed by the parties, as well as their debts and liabilities. The attorney will provide the client with the form for the Inventory.

-J-

JUDGMENT or RULING: A court's decision.

JURISDICTION: The authority of the court to hear a case.

-L-

LIABILITIES: Everything owed by you or your spouse, including mortgages, credit cards or other loans.

-M-

MARKET VALUE: Market value is the most common measure of value. It is defined as the amount a willing buyer who desires to buy but is under no obligation to buy would pay to a willing seller who desires to sell but is under no obligation to sell.

MEDIATOR: A person trained to assist parties in reaching an agreement before going to court. Mediators do not take either party's side and do not give legal advice. They are only responsible for helping the parties reach an agreement and putting that agreement into writing. In most courts, mediation of family law cases is required before going to court.

MOTION: A request made to the court, other than a petition.

-N-

NO-FAULT DIVORCE: In Texas, the court may grant a divorce without regard to the fault of the marriage. However, a spouse may also seek a divorce on the basis of the other spouse's fault, such as cruelty or adultery. Fault grounds are generally pleaded to obtain a disproportionate division of the community estate or to assist in a custody dispute.

-O-

OBJECTION: Notice to the judge by one attorney that the proceedings are objectionable for some reason and the attorneys wants to bring it to the attention of the judge and request a ruling.

OBLIGEE: A person to whom money, such as child support or alimony, is owed.

OBLIGOR: A person who is ordered by the court to pay money, such as child support or alimony.

OPENING STATEMENT: A brief statement by an attorney of his client's version of the facts and position on the issues and applicable law, generally at the beginning of the trial.

ORDER: A written decision signed by a judge and filed in the case record that contains the judge's decision on some part of a case, usually on a motion.

OVERRULED: When an attorney objects to something said or done in the courtroom, this means the judge disagrees with the objecting attorney.

-P-

PARENTING COURSE: Teaches parents how to coparent, help their children cope with divorce and other family issues. Often ordered by the courts in divorce actions for parties with children.

PARTY: A person involved in a court case, either as a petitioner or respondent.

PATERNITY (PARENTAGE) ACTION: A lawsuit used to determine whether a designated individual is the father of a specific child or children.

PETITIONER: The person who files the legal paper that begins a court case.

PLEADINGS: The legal documents filed in court, such as the Original Petition for Divorce and Original Answer.

POSTNUPTIAL (POSTMARITAL) AGREEMENT: A postnuptial agreement is an agreement between spouses to partition or exchange any part of their community property to a spouse's separate property.

PRENUPTIAL (PREMARITAL) AGREEMENT: Also called a "prenup," this is an agreement between prospective spouses made in contemplation of marriage and to be effective on marriage. Premarital agreements allow persons about to marry to confirm and modify the characterization of property.

PRIMARY RESIDENCE: The home in which the children spend most of their time.

PROCESS SERVER: Person who serves legal papers on those being sued.

PRO SE LITIGANT: A person who appears in court without the assistance of a lawyer.

-Q-

QUALIFIED DOMESTIC RELATIONS ORDER: Called a Quadro, the most common use is for the division of retirement benefits on divorce. The QDRO is an order signed by the judge directed to a retirement plan administrator which permits a non-employee former spouse to receive his or her share of retirement benefits directly.

-R-

RESPONDENT: The person who is served with a petition for divorce.

RETIREMENT BENEFITS – DEFINED BENEFIT PLAN: A defined benefit plan promises employees a monthly benefit beginning at retirement, and calculates the benefit factors specific to each plan, such as years of service, age and salary.

RETIREMENT BENEFITS – DEFINED CONTRIBUTION PLAN: An employee participating in a defined contribution plan has an individual account to which generally both the employer and the employee make contributions.

-S-

SEPARATE PROPERTY: A spouse's separate property consists of property owned or claimed by the spouse before marriage; property acquired by a spouse during marriage by gift or inheritance; and recovery for personal injuries sustained by the spouse during marriage, except for any recovery for loss of earning capacity during marriage. A court cannot divest a spouse of his or her separate property in dividing the marital estate on divorce. A spouse claiming that disputed property is his or her separate property must prove that the property is separate property by clear and convincing evidence. Income from separate property in Texas is community property.

SERVICE: When a copy of a divorce petition (or other pleading) that has been filed by the court is delivered by a constable or private process server to the other party.

SETTLEMENT AGREEMENT: A document that sets out the agreement between the two parties when a divorce is settled.

SOCIAL STUDY: A report based on a study of the parties' home life that is filed with the court indicating what is in the best interests of children. The study is conducted by a neutral person who may be agreed by the parties or appointed by the court to evaluate or investigate your child's situation.

SPOUSAL MAINTENANCE: Payments to be made by one spouse to another spouse for a limited period of time to allow one of the parties an opportunity to complete a plan of education or training, so that he or she may better support himself or herself. Except for a spouse with an incapacitating disability, a court may not order maintenance that remains in effect for more than three years after the date of the order. Further, a court may not order maintenance that requires a spouse to pay each month more than $2,500 or 20% of the spouse's average gross monthly income.

STOCK OPTION: The right to buy a designated stock at anytime within a specified period at a determinable price, if the holder of the option chooses. Stock options may be vested or unvested.

SUBPOENA: A document served on a person, requiring an appearance at a certain time and place to testify and/or bring designated documents.

-T-

TEMPORARY INJUNCTION: The purpose of a temporary injunction is to preserve the status quo during the pendency of the case. The injunction prohibits the spouses from doing or failing to do certain things, such as prohibiting the parties from spending funds in an amount in excess of reasonable and necessary living expenses, and preventing the dissipation, destruction or transfer of the parties' property during the pendency of the proceeding.

TEMPORARY ORDERS: Temporary orders entered during the divorce case can accomplish many things, including award the occupancy of the marital home to one of the parties, establish temporary custody and visitation of the parties' children, direct payment of temporary spousal or child support, direct a party to pay interim attorney's fees and direct the parties to provide an inventory and appraisement of their property.

TEMPORARY RESTRAINING ORDER: When a divorce suit has been filed, the court may, without notice to the other party, grant a temporary restraining order to preserve and protect the parties' property. Such an order may prohibit a party from spending money or withdrawing funds other than for reasonable and necessary living expenses, business expenses and attorney's fees. The temporary restraining order lasts for 14 days, unless an extension is granted, and is typically turned into a temporary injunction that is applicable to both parties.

TRACING: Involves establishing the separate origin of the property through evidence showing the time and means by which the spouse originally obtained possession of the property. Because all property possessed by either spouse on divorce is presumed to be community property, a party making a separate property claim must trace and clearly identify the claimed separate property. Separate property will retain its character through a series of exchanges so long as the party asserting separate ownership can overcome the presumption of community property by tracing the assets during marriage back to property that is separate property. For example, when separate funds can be traced through a bank account to specific property purchased with those funds, then the property purchased is also separate.

TRIAL: The final hearing that decides all issues in a contested case.

-V-

VALUATION: The process by which the value of an asset is determined. Before a court can divide the property, it must have evidence of the value of the property. The court may consider various types of evidence in determining the value of the parties' community property. Evidence of property values can come from financial statements, tax returns, expert testimony, formal appraisals, inventories of the parties, and the testimony of the parties.

VENUE: The jurisdiction where the case is heard.

-W-

WAIVER OF CITATION: If the respondent does not wish to be formally served with the citation in a divorce, he or she may sign a Waiver of Citation acknowledging receipt of a copy of the final divorce petition.

Appendix C

Texas Family Code
Subchapter C. Child Support Guidelines

§ 154.121. Guidelines for the Support of a Child

The child support guidelines in this subchapter are intended to guide the court in determining an equitable amount of child support.

Added by Acts 1995, 74th Leg., ch. 20, § 1, eff. April 20, 1995.

§ 154.122. Application of Guidelines Rebuttably Presumed in Best Interest of Child

(a) The amount of a periodic child support payment established by the child support guidelines in effect in this state at the time of the hearing is presumed to be reasonable, and an order of support conforming to the guidelines is presumed to be in the best interest of the child.

(b) A court may determine that the application of the guidelines would be unjust or inappropriate under the circumstances.

Added by Acts 1995, 74th Leg., ch. 20, § 1, eff. April 20, 1995.

§ 154.123. Additional Factors for Court to Consider

(a) The court may order periodic child support payments in an amount other than that established by the guidelines if the evidence rebuts the presumption that application of the guidelines is in the best interest of the child and justifies a variance from the guidelines.

(b) In determining whether application of the guidelines would be unjust or inappropriate under the circumstances, the court shall consider evidence of all relevant factors, including:

(1) the age and needs of the child;

(2) the ability of the parents to contribute to the support of the child;

(3) any financial resources available for the support of the child;

(4) the amount of time of possession of and access to a child;

(5) the amount of the obligee's net resources, including the earning potential of the obligee if the actual income of the obligee is significantly less than what the obligee could earn because the obligee is intentionally unemployed or underemployed and including an increase or decrease in the income of the obligee or income that may be attributed to the property and assets of the obligee;

(6) child care expenses incurred by either party in order to maintain gainful employment;

(7) whether either party has the managing conservatorship or actual physical custody of another child;

(8) the amount of alimony or spousal maintenance actually and currently being paid or received by a party;

(9) the expenses for a son or daughter for education beyond secondary school;

(10) whether the obligor or obligee has an automobile, housing, or other benefits furnished by his or her employer, another person, or a business entity;

(11) the amount of other deductions from the wage or salary income and from other compensation for personal services of the parties;

(12) provision for health care insurance and payment of uninsured medical expenses;

(13) special or extraordinary educational, health care, or other expenses of the parties or of the child;

(14) the cost of travel in order to exercise possession of and access to a child;

(15) positive or negative cash flow from any real and personal property and assets, including a business and investments;

(16) debts or debt service assumed by either party; and

(17) any other reason consistent with the best interest of the child, taking into consideration the circumstances of the parents.

Added by Acts 1995, 74th Leg., ch. 20, § 1, eff. April 20, 1995.

§ 154.124. Agreement Concerning Support

(a) To promote the amicable settlement of disputes between the parties to a suit, the parties may enter into a written agreement containing provisions for support of the child and for modification of the agreement, including variations from the child support guidelines provided by Subchapter C.

(b) If the court finds that the agreement is in the child's best interest, the court shall render an order in accordance with the agreement.

(c) Terms of the agreement in the order may be enforced by

all remedies available for enforcement of a judgment, including contempt, but are not enforceable as contract terms unless provided by the agreement.

(d) If the court finds the agreement is not in the child's best interest, the court may request the parties to submit a revised agreement or the court may render an order for the support of the child.

Added by Acts 1995, 74th Leg., ch. 20, § 1, eff. April 20, 1995.

§ 154.125. Application of Guidelines to Net Resources of $6,000 or Less

(a) The guidelines for the support of a child in this section are specifically designed to apply to situations in which the obligor's monthly net resources are $6,000 or less.

(b) If the obligor's monthly net resources are $6,000 or less, the court shall presumptively apply the following schedule in rendering the child support order:

CHILD SUPPORT GUIDELINES BASED ON THE
MONTHLY NET RESOURCES OF THE OBLIGOR

1 child	20% of Obligor's Net Resources
2 children	25% of Obligor's Net Resources
3 children	30% of Obligor's Net Resources
4 children	35% of Obligor's Net Resources
5 children	40% of Obligor's Net Resources
6+ children	Not less than the amount for 5 children

Added by Acts 1995, 74th Leg., ch. 20, § 1, eff. April 20, 1995.

§ 154.126. Application of Guidelines to Net Resources of More Than $6,000 Monthly

(a) If the obligor's net resources exceed $6,000 per month, the court shall presumptively apply the percentage guidelines to the first $6,000 of the obligor's net resources. Without further reference to the percentage recommended by these guidelines, the court may order additional amounts of child support as appropriate, depending on the income of the parties and the proven needs of the child.

(b) The proper calculation of a child support order that exceeds the presumptive amount established for the first $6,000 of the obligor's net resources requires that the entire amount of the presumptive award be subtracted from the proven total needs of the child. After the presumptive award is subtracted, the court shall allocate between the parties the responsibility to meet the additional needs of the child according to the circumstances of the parties. However, in no event may the obligor be required to pay more child support than the greater of the presumptive amount or the amount equal to 100 percent of the proven needs of the child.

Added by Acts 1995, 74th Leg., ch. 20, § 1, eff. April 20, 1995.

§ 154.127. Partial Termination of Support Obligation

A child support order for more than one child shall provide that, on the termination of support for a child, the level of support for the remaining child or children is in accordance with the child support guidelines.

Added by Acts 1995, 74th Leg., ch. 20, § 1, eff. April 20, 1995.

§ 154.128. Computing Support for Children in More Than One Household

(a) In applying the child support guidelines for an obligor who has children in more than one household, the court shall apply the percentage guidelines in this subchapter by making the following computation:

(1) determine the amount of child support that would be ordered if all children whom the obligor has the legal duty to support lived in one household by applying the schedule in this subchapter;

(2) compute a child support credit for the obligor's children who are not before the court by dividing the amount determined under Subdivision (1) by the total number of children whom the obligor is obligated to support and multiplying that number by the number of the obligor's children who are not before the court;

(3) determine the adjusted net resources of the obligor by subtracting the child support credit computed under Subdivision (2) from the net resources of the obligor; and

(4) determine the child support amount for the children before the court by applying the percentage guidelines for one household for the number of children of the obligor before the court to the obligor's adjusted net resources.

(b) For the purpose of determining a child support credit, the total number of an obligor's children includes the children before the court for the establishment or modification of a support order and any other children, including children residing with the obligor, whom the obligor has the legal duty of support.

(c) The child support credit with respect to children for whom the obligor is obligated by an order to pay support is computed, regardless of whether the obligor is delinquent in child support payments, without regard to the amount of the order.

Added by Acts 1995, 74th Leg., ch. 20, § 1, eff. April 20, 1995.

§ 154.129. Alternative Method of Computing Support for Children in More Than One Household

In lieu of performing the computation under the preceding section, the court may determine the child support amount for the children before the court by applying the percentages in the table below to the obligor's net resources:

MULTIPLE FAMILY ADJUSTED GUIDELINES
(% OF NET RESOURCES)

Number of children before the court

	1	2	3	4	5	6	7
Number of other children for whom the obligor has a duty of support							
0	20.00	25.00	30.00	35.00	40.00	40.00	40.00
1	17.50	22.50	27.38	32.20	37.33	37.71	38.00
2	16.00	20.63	25.20	30.33	35.43	36.00	36.44
3	14.75	19.00	24.00	29.00	34.00	34.67	35.20
4	13.60	18.33	23.14	28.00	32.89	33.60	34.18
5	13.33	17.86	22.50	27.22	32.00	32.73	33.33
6	13.14	17.50	22.00	26.60	31.27	32.00	32.62
7	13.00	17.22	21.60	26.09	30.67	31.38	32.00

Added by Acts 1995, 74th Leg., ch. 20, § 1, eff. April 20, 1995.

§ 154.130. Findings in Child Support Order

(a) Without regard to Rules 296 through 299, Texas Rules of Civil Procedure, in rendering an order of child support, the court shall make the findings required by Subsection (b) if:

(1) a party files a written request with the court not later than 10 days after the date of the hearing;

(2) a party makes an oral request in open court during the hearing; or

(3) the amount of child support ordered by the court varies from the amount computed by applying the percentage guidelines.

(b) If findings are required by this section, the court shall state whether the application of the guidelines would be unjust or inappropriate and shall state the following in the child support order:

"(1) the monthly net resources of the obligor per month are $_____;

"(2) the monthly net resources of the obligee per month are $_____;

"(3) the percentage applied to the obligor's net resources for child support by the actual order rendered by the court is _____%;

"(4) the amount of child support if the percentage guidelines are applied to the first $6,000 of the obligor's net resources is $_____;

"(5) if applicable, the specific reasons that the amount of

child support per month ordered by the court varies from the amount stated in Subdivision (4) are: _____; and

"(6) if applicable, the obligor is obligated to support children in more than one household, and:

"(A) the number of children before the court is _____;

"(B) the number of children not before the court residing in the same household with the obligor is _____; and

"(C) the number of children not before the court for whom the obligor is obligated by a court order to pay support, without regard to whether the obligor is delinquent in child support payments, and who are not counted under Paragraph (A) or (B) is _____."

(c) The application of the guidelines under Section 154.129 does not constitute a variance from the child support guidelines requiring specific findings by the court under this section.

Added by Acts 1995, 74th Leg., ch. 20, § 1, eff. April 20, 1995.

Amended by Acts 2001, 77th Leg., ch. 1023, § 8, eff. Sept. 1, 2001.

§ 154.131. Retroactive Child Support

(a) The child support guidelines are intended to guide the court in determining the amount of retroactive child support, if any, to be ordered.

(b) In ordering retroactive child support, the court shall consider the net resources of the obligor during the relevant time period and whether:

(1) the mother of the child had made any previous attempts to

notify the obligor of his paternity or probable paternity;

(2) the obligor had knowledge of his paternity or probable paternity;

(3) the order of retroactive child support will impose an undue financial hardship on the obligor or the obligor's family; and

(4) the obligor has provided actual support or other necessaries before the filing of the action.

(c) It is presumed that a court order limiting the amount of retroactive child support to an amount that does not exceed the total amount of support that would have been due for the four years preceding the date the petition seeking support was filed is reasonable and in the best interest of the child.

(d) The presumption created under this section may be rebutted by evidence that the obligor:

(1) knew or should have known that the obligor was the father of the child for whom support is sought; and

(2) sought to avoid the establishment of a support obligation to the child.

(e) An order under this section limiting the amount of retroactive support does not constitute a variance from the guidelines requiring the court to make specific findings under Section 154.130.

Added by Acts 1995, 74th Leg., ch. 20, § 1, eff. April 20, 1995.

Amended by Acts 2001, 77th Leg., ch. 392, § 1, eff. Sept. 1, 2001; Acts 2001, 77th Leg., ch. 821, § 2.14, eff. June 14, 2001; Acts 2001, 77th Leg., ch. 1023, § 9, eff. Sept. 1, 2001.

§ 154.132. Application of Guidelines to Children of Certain Disabled Obligors

In applying the child support guidelines for an obligor who has a disability and who is required to pay support for a child who receives benefits as a result of the obligor's disability, the court shall apply the guidelines by determining the amount of child support that would be ordered under the child support guidelines and subtracting from that total the amount of benefits or the value of the benefits paid to or for the child as a result of the obligor's disability.

Added by Acts 1999, 76th Leg., ch. 891, § 1, eff. Sept. 1, 1999.

§ 154.133. Application of Guidelines to Children of Obligors Receiving Social Security

In applying the child support guidelines for an obligor who is receiving social security old age benefits and who is required to pay support for a child who receives benefits as a result of the obligor's receipt of social security old age benefits, the court shall apply the guidelines by determining the amount of child support that would be ordered under the child support guidelines and subtracting from that total the amount of benefits or the value of the benefits paid to or for the child as a result of the obligor's receipt of social security old age benefits.

Added by Acts 2001, 77th Leg., ch. 544, § 1, eff. Sept. 1, 2001.

Appendix D

PREPARING FOR YOUR DEPOSITION

I.   WHAT IS A DEPOSITION?

A deposition is a commonly used pretrial discovery device. You, as the deponent, are placed under oath and will answer questions asked by your spouse's attorney in front of a court reporter. The questions and answers will be recorded by the court reporter who will prepare a written transcript of the deposition. Your deposition may also be videotaped.

Your deposition must be taken seriously, as you will be testifying in your deposition just as if you were testifying in court.

II.   PURPOSE OF A DEPOSITION

The main reasons for a deposition are as follows:

A. Your spouse's attorney wants to find out your knowledge regarding the issues in your divorce action. He or she is interested in what your story is now and what it is going to be at trial.

B. Your spouse's attorney wants to size up your demeanor and determine what type of witness you will make at trial.

C. Your spouse's attorney wants to nail down your version of the facts before trial so that they know in advance what your testimony will be at trial.

D. Your spouse's attorney wants to catch you in a lie or an omission that can be used at trial to show that you are not honest and cast doubt on the veracity of your testimony. The transcript of your deposition may be used at trial by the opposing attorney to point out any trial testimony that varies from your deposition testimony.

Your spouse's attorney has every right to take your deposition. Your attorney also has the right to ask questions of you during the deposition, but most often your attorney will only ask questions to clarify an answer that may have been misleading or confusing.

Avoid the natural tendency to launch into your entire version of the case. This is not the proper time or place. Briefly and concisely answer only the question asked.

The testimony given in your deposition can be used in the trial of your case. A well-done deposition can have a positive effect on your case — the opposing attorney can see that you are an excellent witness and that you have a good case. Your chances of settlement will then be greatly improved.

III.   WHO WILL BE PRESENT AT THE DEPOSITION

Depositions are usually taken in a conference room at the opposing attorney's office. The people typically in attendance are the parties, their attorneys and the court reporter. Spouses of the parties may also attend the deposition. Occasionally, a legal assistant will be present at the deposition. No judge is present.

IV.   LENGTH OF DEPOSITION

The length of your deposition will depend on the complexity of the issues in your case, as well as the number of questions opposing counsel asks you. Do not make any other appointments or commitments on the day of your deposition. Under the Texas Rules of Civil Procedure, an individual may not be deposed for more than 6 hours. Breaks during the depositions do not count against this limitation.

V.   QUESTIONS ASKED

Under the Texas Rules of Civil Procedure, attorneys have the right to ask a number of questions. Some of the topics discussed at your deposition will not be admissible at trial. Unless your attorney instructs you not to answer a particular question, you must answer the question, even if your attorney objects to the question.

While opposing counsel may act like your friend in order to get you to relax and trust him or her, do not let your guard down. On the other hand, opposing counsel may try to wear you down by being confrontational, relentless and harassing. Regardless of the technique used, always be on guard and maintain a calm composure.

VI.   OBJECTIONS BY YOUR ATTORNEY

Your attorney will protect you from any improper questions by opposing counsel. Rarely will your attorney ask you any questions. The objections that can be made during the deposition are (1) leading, (2) form and (3) nonresponsive. Attorneys may also object and instruct the witness not to answer questions seeking privileged information. If the opposing attorney asks an improper question, your attorney may make an objection (e.g., "I object to the question on the ground of attorney-client privilege."). If your attorney ever instructs you not to answer a question, do not answer the question.

VII. HOW SHOULD I DRESS?

Your personal appearance should be conservative, neat, clean, and comfortable. Business or business casual attire is appropriate. Your appearance should indicate that you are taking this matter and your deposition seriously. If your deposition will be videotaped, it is especially important for you to dress appropriately.

VIII. THE COURT REPORTER'S ROLE

The court reporter is present to administer the oath (under which you swear to tell the truth) and record everything that you, the opposing attorney and your attorney say during the deposition. The court reporter is neutral and does not decide or mediate any disputes between the attorneys or parties. After the deposition, the court reporter prepares a written transcript of your deposition testimony and sends it to the attorneys.

IX. PREPARING FOR YOUR DEPOSITION

A. Review the Pleadings and Discovery Responses

In preparing for your deposition, review all of the pleadings filed in your case, as well as any affidavits, motions and discovery responses. Make sure that you understand all of the allegations, requests, causes of action and/or defenses raised in these documents.

B. Gather Any Requested Documents

You may have been requested to bring documents to your deposition. If the notice of your deposition includes a document request, you must gather documents, review them with your attorney and bring them to your deposition. If you have not been asked to bring documents to your deposition, do not bring anything. Leave your briefcase, calendar, PDA, etc., at home. You are not required to, and should not bring, any documents that you are not expressly requested to bring. Even if you think that a particular document is important, discuss the matter with your attorney before bringing it to your deposition.

Letters and e-mail between you and your attorney or his or her staff, and any memos or other documents prepared solely by your attorney or his staff, or prepared by you at the request of and for your attorney, are usually protected by law from being disclosed under the "attorney-client privilege" and the "work-product privilege." You should not produce such documents. If it appears to you that the request for documents would include documents that are privileged and confidential, bring this to the attention of your attorney.

If a document has not been requested, do not agree to supply documents or information. If you are asked to supply documents or information, refer the request to your counsel.

C. Conference with Your Attorney

Before the deposition, you and your attorney will have a conference to discuss the documents you are to bring to your deposition and what you can expect during your deposition. It is important that you be totally candid and tell the complete truth to your attorney, even if it appears to be damaging to your case.

It is okay to admit in your deposition that you have met and consulted with your attorney prior to your deposition. Anything that you and your attorney discuss is confidential and should not be revealed to the other side. If the opposing attorney asks you a question that your attorney believes you should not answer as it is an attorney-client communication, your attorney will object to the question and instruct you not to answer it.

Private conferences with your attorney during the deposition are improper except to determine if a privilege should be asserted, although they may be held during agreed recesses and adjournments.

X.   ANSWERING QUESTIONS

A. Give Truthful and Accurate Testimony

In responding to the questions you are asked, you should always give truthful and accurate testimony. At the beginning of your deposition, you take an oath to tell the truth. You must tell the truth even if it is damaging to your case. If your testimony is not truthful and accurate, opposing counsel can later use your testimony against you at trial. Further, failure to tell the truth in a deposition constitutes perjury, which is a crime in Texas.

The following tips will help you give truthful and accurate testimony:

1.Your answers must be based upon your personal knowledge. Never volunteer your opinion unless expressly asked to do so. Never guess or speculate about a fact. If you did not personally witness or observe something, then you are justified in saying that you do not know the answer, even though you may have heard second hand facts or information. Additionally, if you are asked why a certain decision was made but you did not participate in making the decision, you should say that you do not know why the decision was made. Similarly, do not speculate as to what "probably" happened. Your deposition testimony should rest upon first hand knowledge and a clear memory, not upon hearsay or speculation.

2. If you do not know the answer to a question, say so. If you cannot remember, say so.

3. If you are not sure of a particular fact, qualify your answer by beginning "to the best of my recollection."

4. Do not let opposing counsel put words in your mouth. If the opposing attorney attempts to summarize facts or testimony, listen very carefully to his or her summary and do not agree with it unless it is completely accurate. If it is not, simply state that you do not agree with the summary. If the introductory clause to a question contains any inaccurate information, be certain to specify the inaccurate information contained in the question prior to answering the question. If the question asked calls for a "yes" or "no" answer, and that type of answer does not accurately reflect the facts, you are not required to answer only "yes" or "no." Indicate that you are unable to do this.

5. Do not be intimidated by insinuations by the opposing attorney regarding your lack of truthfulness. If the attorney says, "You mean to tell me that you are willing to sit here under oath and swear to that fact?," remain calm, look the attorney in the eye and say, "I have just testified to that fact under oath."

6. Be careful of questions that ask "is that all?" It is okay to say "to the best of my knowledge at this time."

7. You may be asked a question like: "Tell me all of the negative qualities of your spouse as a parent." The lawyer asking the question is trying to put you in a box and limit you at trial to what your answer was in your deposition. If you are asked this type of question, give as many reasons as you can, but when you finish, give yourself an escape route out of the box by saying, "I am sure there are other reasons, but I cannot think of them right now." Another way an attorney will try to put a box around your testimony is to ask you to tell everything you can remember about a certain event. Always leave yourself an exit route out of the box by saying, "That is all I can remember at this time."

8. Be careful about events that happened a long time ago. For example, if you are asked about some event that occurred many years ago, and you do not remember the exact time or date, simply say so. Do not guess.

9. You can phrase your answers at times in a manner that may be helpful to your case. For example, instead of simply saying "yes," a more heart-felt response might be "of course" or "absolutely."

10. Avoid using "always" and "never."

11. If opposing counsel asks you about certain documents, you may ask to see the document before you answer the questions. When confronted with documents, examine them carefully. If you haven't seen a particular document before or did not prepare it, don't try to guess what it means. Do not vouch for the accuracy of someone else's document.

12. If at any time during the deposition you realize you have given an erroneous answer, correct your answer as soon as you recognize your error.

13. Watch our for compound questions.

14. If your testimony is based upon an approximation, you should make this clear to the examining lawyer. Any testimony that is based on estimates should be given only where the record unequivocally reflects that this is the basis for the testimony.

15. Do not guess details. Be careful of giving exact information (such as measurements, dates, time intervals and business statistics) if you are uncertain about the details, particularly when the information is available in some business or other records. If you are asked a question of this nature and you are uncertain, respond that you do not remember the exact information. If the information requested is available from certain records, you may add that any answer you give will be your best estimate only, and is subject to verification through applicable records.

B. Listen to the Question and Make Sure you Understand It.

Listen to the question carefully and make sure you understand it before you answer. Pause for a few seconds before responding to each question to make sure that you understand the question and think about the answer. If you did not hear or understand the question, politely inform the opposing counsel to repeat or explain the question.

C. Do Not Volunteer Information

Answer the question you are asked as concisely as possible and then stop. Give as short an answer as possible, and be sure your response is narrowed to the exact question asked. There is usually no benefit to volunteering information. Your deposition is not the time to tell your side of the story.

Following are some tips for answering questions without volunteering information:

1. Do not give your opinion regarding any fact or issue unless you are asked for your opinion—just answer the question that you are asked.

2. If the opposing counsel asks you a question that calls for a "yes" or "no" answer, simply answer "yes" or "no."

3. Avoid rambling answers—do not explain details unless you are requested to do so.

4. Even if the opposing attorney pauses as though he or she is waiting for you to give an explanation, stop talking and wait for the next question.

5. Do not try to anticipate the answer to the next question that you will be asked.

6. Do not voluntarily offer information to the opposing attorney as to where he or she can find information being inquired about unless expressly asked to do so.

7. Do not refer to or volunteer to provide any documents unless expressly requested to do so.

8. Do not let opposing counsel interrupt your full answer. If this happens, politely state that you were not through with your answer and ask if you may finish it.

XI.   **THINGS TO AVOID**

A. Avoid Becoming Nervous or Flustered.
Remember that the opposing attorney is sizing up your

demeanor as a witness during your deposition (which may greatly affect settlement negotiations). Therefore, your conduct, appearance and demeanor at your deposition is important. It is important to present a good impression. You should try to relax, remain calm and not appear nervous. Speak loudly and positively and with self assurance. There is no need to show fear or anxiety or be afraid to answer truthfully.

B. Avoid Getting Angry or Mad.

It is important that you conduct yourself in a reasonable and mature fashion during your deposition. Avoid losing your temper, getting mad or upset, cursing or engaging in name calling. Opposing counsel may try to provoke you so that you hurt your case—do not let this happen. Your conduct should be polite, courteous and calm. Do not interrupt opposing counsel's questions. Never argue with opposing counsel.

C. Avoid Humor.

Avoid all jokes or wisecracks in a deposition. What may at the time seem like an innocent joke may not appear to be a joking matter in the written transcript. Never try to get the upper hand on the opposing attorney by using some clever comeback or by turning the tables and asking him or her questions.

D. Avoid Referring to Documents.

Never refer to any document to refresh your memory unless you have been authorized to do so by your attorney. A rule of law in Texas is that if a deponent is asked a question, and he or she stops and looks at a document in order to refresh his memory, then that document is required to be disclosed and handed over to the opposing attorney.

XII. <u>READING AND SIGNING THE DEPOSITION</u>

After your deposition is concluded, the court reporter will transcribe the record into a typed written deposition transcript. You will then be given an opportunity to read the deposition and make corrections, either in misspellings, mistaken dates or other such changes. You will also need to give a reason for each such change.

Appendix E

Post-Divorce Checklist

Checklist	Needs to be Done	Completed
Appeal Deadline: 42 days from entry of Final Judgment of Divorce		
Prepare Deeds and File		
Real Property Deeds		
Estate Documents		
Will		
Medical Directive		
Power of Attorney		
Name Change (Probate Court)		
Automobile Titles		
Automobile Insurance		
Insurance Forms		
Life Insurance Provisions - Notify Carrier of Beneficiary Change		
Health Insurance Provisions - Notify carrier and order new identification card(s)		
Bank Accounts		
Safety Deposit Box		
Tax-IRS Forms		
IRS Form 8332 (Dependency Exemption)		
Form W-4		
Retirement Accounts / IRA / Pension		
QDRO		
Income Withholding Orders		

Appendix F

IRS FORM 8332 -- DEPENDENT EXEMPTION

Form **8332** (Rev. December 2000) Department of the Treasury Internal Revenue Service	**Release of Claim to Exemption** **for Child of Divorced or Separated Parents** ▶ **Attach** to noncustodial parent's return **each year** exemption is claimed. **Caution:** *Do not use this form if you were never married.*	OMB No. 1545-0915 Attachment Sequence No. **115**
Name of noncustodial parent claiming exemption		Noncustodial parent's social security number (SSN) ▶

Part I   **Release of Claim to Exemption for Current Year**

I agree not to claim an exemption for_____
                                              Name(s) of child (or children)

for the tax year 20_____ .

_____   _____   _____
      Signature of custodial parent releasing claim to exemption   Custodial parent's SSN   Date

Note: *If you choose not to claim an exemption for this child (or children) for future tax years, also complete Part II.*

Part II   **Release of Claim to Exemption for Future Years** (If completed, see **Noncustodial parent** below.)

I agree not to claim an exemption for_____
                                              Name(s) of child (or children)

for the tax year(s)_____ .
                    (Specify. See instructions.)

_____   _____   _____
      Signature of custodial parent releasing claim to exemption   Custodial parent's SSN   Date

General Instructions

Purpose of form. If you are a **custodial parent** and you were ever married to the child's **noncustodial parent**, you may use this form to release your claim to your child's exemption. To do so, complete this form (or a similar statement containing the same information required by this form) and give it to the noncustodial parent who will claim the child's exemption. The noncustodial parent must attach this form or similar statement to his or her tax return **each year** the exemption is claimed.

You are the **custodial parent** if you had custody of the child for most of the year. You are the **noncustodial parent** if you had custody for a shorter period of time or did not have custody at all. For the definition of custody, see **Pub. 501,** Exemptions, Standard Deduction, and Filing Information.

Support test for children of divorced or separated parents. Generally, the custodial parent is treated as having provided over half of the child's support if:

• The child received over half of his or her total support for the year from one or both of the parents **and**

• The child was in the custody of one or both of the parents for more than half of the year.

Note: *Public assistance payments, such as Temporary Assistance for Needy Families (TANF), are not support provided by the parents.*

For this support test to apply, the parents must be one of the following:

• Divorced or legally separated under a decree of divorce or separate maintenance,

• Separated under a written separation agreement, **or**

• Living apart at all times during the last 6 months of the year.

Caution: *This support test does not apply to parents who never married each other.*

If the support test applies, and the other four dependency tests in your tax return

instruction booklet are also met, the custodial parent can claim the child's exemption.

Exception. The custodial parent will not be treated as having provided over half of the child's support if **any** of the following apply.

• The custodial parent agrees not to claim the child's exemption by signing this form or similar statement.

• The child is treated as having received over half of his or her total support from a person under a multiple support agreement (**Form 2120,** Multiple Support Declaration).

• A pre-1985 divorce decree or written separation agreement states that the noncustodial parent can claim the child as a dependent. But the noncustodial parent must provide at least $600 for the child's support during the year. This rule does not apply if the decree or agreement was changed after 1984 to say that the noncustodial parent cannot claim the child as a dependent.

Additional information. For more details, see **Pub. 504,** Divorced or Separated Individuals.

Specific Instructions

Custodial parent. You may agree to release your claim to the child's exemption for the current tax year or for future years, or both.

• Complete **Part I** if you agree to release your claim to the child's exemption for the current tax year.

• Complete **Part II** if you agree to release your claim to the child's exemption for any or all future years. If you do, write the specific future year(s) or "all future years" in the space provided in Part II.

 To help ensure future support, you may not want to release your claim to the child's exemption for future years.

Noncustodial parent. Attach this form or similar statement to your tax return for **each year** you claim the child's exemption. You may claim the exemption **only** if the other four dependency tests in your tax return instruction booklet are met.

Note: *If the custodial parent released his or her claim to the child's exemption for any future year, you **must** attach a copy of this form or similar statement to your tax return for each future year that you claim the exemption. Keep a copy for your records.*

Paperwork Reduction Act Notice. We ask for the information on this form to carry out the Internal Revenue laws of the United States. You are required to give us the information. We need it to ensure that you are complying with these laws and to allow us to figure and collect the right amount of tax.

You are not required to provide the information requested on a form that is subject to the Paperwork Reduction Act unless the form displays a valid OMB control number. Books or records relating to a form or its instructions must be retained as long as their contents may become material in the administration of any Internal Revenue law. Generally, tax returns and return information are confidential, as required by Internal Revenue Code section 6103.

The time needed to complete and file this form will vary depending on individual circumstances. The estimated average time is:

Recordkeeping	. 7 min.
Learning about the law or the form	. 5 min.
Preparing the form	. 7 min.
Copying, assembling, and sending the form to the IRS	. . 14 min.

If you have comments concerning the accuracy of these time estimates or suggestions for making this form simpler, we would be happy to hear from you. You can write to the Tax Forms Committee, Western Area Distribution Center, Rancho Cordova, CA 95743-0001. **Do not** send the form to this address. Instead, see the instructions for Form 1040 or Form 1040A.

Cat. No. 13910F   Form **8332** (Rev. 12-2000)

Appendix G

CREDIT REPORT REQUEST LETTER

The address of local and national credit bureau reporting firms is found in the Yellow Pages.

Name
Address
City, State, Zip

Date

Credit Bureau
Address
City, State Zip

Re: [First] [Middle Initial] [Maiden] [Last]
        SSN

This is to request that a copy of my entire credit history/report be mailed to me at the above address. I have enclosed a check in the amount of $_____ to cover the cost of the report and shipping.

Thank you in advance for your prompt response to my request.

Very truly yours,

[Name]

Co-Authors (from left) Heather King, Ike Vanden Eykel, Rick Robertson and Charla Bradshaw Conner are among America's most outstanding family law attorneys.

Each has been selected a Texas Super Lawyer in a survey of their peers. Ike has been honored among the top 10 divorce lawyers in America and Rick has been named one of the top lawyers in Dallas/Fort Worth. Heather and Charla are among the top 50 women attorneys in Texas. This is Ike's fourth book.

All are available to speak to groups avout the financial aspects of divorce and other family law-related issues. Call Kim Hyde at 972/769-2727 or email heather@koonsfuller.com, ike@koonsfuller.com, rick@koonsfuller.com or charla@koonsfuller.com.